MW01027098

PADRE PIO'S SPIRITUAL DIRECTION FOR EVERY DAY

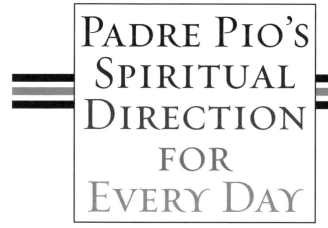

PADRE PIO'S SPIRITUAL DIRECTION FOR EVERY DAY

GIANLUIGI PASQUALE

TRANSLATED BY MARSHA DAIGLE-WILLIAMSON

SERVANT
BOOKS

PUBLISHED BY ST. ANTHONY MESSENGER PRESS
CINCINNATI, OHIO

Originally published in Italian as *365 Giorni con Padre Pio* by Edizioni San Paolo
S.R.L.–Cinisello Balsamo (MI)

Cover and book design by Mark Sullivan
Cover illustration by Celia Baker

LIBRARY OF CONGRESS CATALOGING-IN-PUBLICATION DATA
Pio, of Pietrelcina, Saint, 1887–1968.
[Correspondence. English. Selections]
Padre Pio's spiritual direction for every day / edited by Gianluigi Pasquale;
translated by Marsha Daigle-Williamson.
p. cm.
Includes bibliographical references.
ISBN 978-1-61636-005-4 (alk. paper)
1. Spiritual life—Catholic Church. 2. Pio, of Pietrelcina, Saint,
1887–1968—Correspondence. 3. Christian saints—Italy—Correspondence.
4. Devotional calendars—Catholic Church. I. Pasquale, Gianluigi. II. Daigle-
Williamson, Marsha. III. Title.
BX2350.3.P5613 2011
242'.2—dc23
2011026128

ISBN 978-1-61636-005-4

Published by Servant Books,
an imprint of St. Anthony Messenger Press.
28 W. Liberty St.
Cincinnati, OH 45202
www.AmericanCatholic.org
www.ServantBooks.org

Printed in the United States of America.
Printed on acid-free paper.

11 12 13 14 15 5 4 3 2 1

CONTENTS

INTRODUCTION

I know many people, especially young people, who pray to God every day through Padre Pio and with Padre Pio. They still think of him as "Padre," even though he has been "St. Pio" of Pietrelcina for some years now. And these people—many in Italy but even more outside Italy—turn to the stigmatic of Gargano on the most ordinary occasions and in the most ordinary circumstances of their daily lives, exhibiting a devotion that manifests itself in several forms: carrying a picture of him in their wallets to show whoever asks them about their faith; displaying his photograph in shops along the superhighways of Italy; and reading extracts from his incomparable letters that have now been collected in volumes.

These letters constitute a very rich mine of Christian spirituality that has not been completely explored. They exhibit a profound love for the humble and the poor, especially for those who work and suffer every day, through whom the history of the world and of salvation moves forward. The letters of Padre Pio speak about God directly to the hearts of readers. They involve correspondence addressed to men and women whom Padre Pio met and listened to for several decades in his confessional—people just like us, needy and never fully satisfied with catching only a glimpse of the wonderful face of Jesus, who has promised to be with us every day until the end of the world (see Matthew 28:20). Padre Pio wrote to these men and women letters that are filled with, among other things, original images and metaphors that are drawn from the most ordinary events of everyday life but that also recall events that occur in nature, scenes of the countryside, and the warmth of affection among family and friends. In a word, he presents the entire fabric of human life that is typically Italian with a wholesome naturalness and straightforward spirituality.

Convinced that Jesus is keeping his promise of being with us each day of every new year, I believe that a "daily thought" taken from the letters of Padre Pio could make Jesus' promise even more tangible. A thought for the day from Padre Pio—and I don't think I am being too bold in affirming this—is a thought for the day for us from Jesus, the one who fully loves and heals us. Both of them were pierced with "the nails of history," the stigmata. This was historically the case for Jesus and occurred through grace for Padre Pio, but for both of them it was physical. The "nails of history" are also "nails," so to speak, that come to people from the breath of the Spirit of God as he leads us day after day to deeper conversion, bringing to maturity in us the wonderful features of the image of Christ (see Ephesians 4:13). Thanks to the Trinitarian passage of time, sooner or later there comes a time of deeper conversion for everybody.

In that sense, such a day did happen for me. I knew almost nothing about Padre Pio except what I had heard, even though I was one of his fellow friars. My discovery of this saint began in Germany several years ago, when I was a student at Sankt Georgen Hochschule (St. George High School), run by the Jesuits in Frankfurt, and a resident guest at the famous and impressive Marian sanctuary Liebfrauen, run by Capuchins in that city. I had been in Germany for a long time. I still remember that cold spring morning in 1999 when the young Father Guardian there, Br. Paulus Terwitte, asked me to give two lectures on Padre Pio, since his beatification was coming up soon that year, on June 16, in Rome. I asked him, "Why me?" He answered, "It is not because you are a Capuchin but because you are an Italian, as Padre Pio was." My hesitation actually did not arise from my having to speak in German in a sanctuary where every Saturday morning—and still today—the best German Catholic and Lutheran theologians give lectures. It arose from my sincere embarrassment that I knew practically nothing about Padre Pio.

I accepted the challenge, however, and that is how I earnestly began to study the sources, that is, the letters that are now being published. I felt as though I had come upon a large vein of gold in an unexplored mine—and not just a theological mine, although it is indeed rich with a precious supply of spiritual intuitions and suggestions that minister great consolation about how to live with and according to the heart of Jesus today. Padre Pio's letters also offer effective advice on how to believe in God, how to hope in the midst of tribulation, how to love and forgive one's neighbor, and how to rejoice in all the circumstances of our lives. The letters pulsate with the vigor of this Capuchin friar who seeks above all to help people be built up in the Christian life, which he considered to be the authentic path to happiness and fulfillment for every human being. In addition, one can trace in these letters the pastoral experience in which he grew as a Franciscan as he directed many souls in the ways of the Spirit. Some of these people he met with only once; others he guided in a very detailed way, in what today we would call spiritual direction.

The thoughts in his letters are addressed to all kinds of people: laypeople, priests, religious, nonbelievers, and young people. In fact, among many discoveries I made, the most fascinating was becoming acquainted through this "diary" of letters with a Padre Pio who was amazingly young and contemporary. I realized this more fully a year later, when I was visiting the locations where he lived in Gargano (in the province of Foggia) and the places of his childhood in Pietrelcina (in Benevento). I became more aware of these qualities in him when I viewed his photographs as a young friar with those large, limpid, and very kind eyes.

Padre Pio always remained young, as we will perceive when listening to him in these thoughts for each day. By the end of the year, we will have been rejuvenated through our reading. This is generally what happens for us as we live out our days in an authentic Christian way: We become aware that "though our outer man is wasting away, our inner man is being renewed every day" (2 Corinthians 4:16). But this is precisely a secret, the one that Padre Pio called "the secret of the great King" (see Tobit 12:7). For a Christian—and not just a Franciscan—the secret coincides exactly with a Person: Jesus.

Venice, Italy
September 23, 2007
Gianluigi Pasquale, O.F.M. CAP.

LETTER RECIPIENTS

Spiritual Directors

Fr. Agostino Daniele (1880–1963) of San Marco in Lamis, teacher of philosophy and sacred eloquence

Fr. Benedetto Nardello (1872–1942) of San Marco in Lamis, teacher of philosophy and physics, expert on mysticism

Spiritual Sons or Friends

Fr. Basilio of Mirabello Sannitico (1889–1965), Franciscan priest at the friary of San Giovanni Rotondo

Luigi Bozzutto (1903–1976), also recipient of letters later as Br. Emmanuele of San Marco la Catola, Franciscan friar at the friary of San Giovanni Rotondo

Br. Gerardo Deliceto (1893–1981), Franciscan friar at the friary of San Giovanni Rotondo

Br. Marcellino Diconsole, Franciscan friar

Franciscan novices

Fr. Paolino di Tomaso (1886–1964) of Casacalenda, friend of Padre Pio at the friary in San Giovanni Rotondo, later provincial

Spiritual Daughters

Elena Bandini (d. 1955), teacher, Third Order Franciscan

Campanile sisters: Maria (1893–1988), schoolteacher, and Lucia

Raffaelina Cerase (1868–1916), wealthy noblewoman, Third Order Franciscan

Lucia Fiorentino (1889–1934), member of the Foggia prayer group

Gargani sisters: Erminia (1883–1962) and Maria (1892–1973) of San Marco la Catola

Girolama Longo, part of a local prayer group

Violante Masone

Graziella Pannullo, schoolteacher, Third Order Franciscan

Annita Rodote (1890–1972), member of the Foggia prayer group, later a nun

Rachelina Russo (1875–1968), member of the Foggia prayer group

Assunta di Tomaso (1894–1953) of Casacalenda, sister of Fr. Paolino

Margherita Tresca (1888–1965) of Barletta, later a nun

Ventrella sisters: Vittoria, Elena, and Filomena

Antonietta Vona (1886–1949)

Other

Pope Paul VI (1897–1978)

SIGNIFICANT DATES RELATED TO CORRESPONDENCE

1903, January 3	joins the Capuchin order at age fifteen
1904, January 22	begins novitiate
1908, December	ordained to minor orders
1910, August 10	ordained to the priesthood at age twenty-three
1910, September 7	experiences pain in hands and feet, which will continue on and off for the next eight years
1911–1916	serves in hometown of Pietrelcina for health reasons
1916, December	reassigned to the friary in San Giovanni Rotondo
1918, August 5	experiences transverberation (mystical piercing of the heart)
1918, September 20	receives stigmata
1923–1933	forbidden to write letters and otherwise restricted

JANUARY

January 1

I heartily recommend that you take concern to have your heart be more pleasing to our Master day by day. Do things in such a way that the current year will be more fruitful in good works than the last. The years are passing by, and we are approaching eternity, so we need to redouble our courage and lift our souls up to God, serving him with more diligence in everything that our Christian vocation or profession requires of us. This alone can make us pleasing to God. It can free us from the world that is not of him and from all our other enemies. Only this can enable us to arrive at the gate of eternal salvation.

Let us then face the present trials to which Divine Providence subjects us, but let us not lose heart or be discouraged. Let us fight hard, and we will carry off the prize that God has stored up for strong souls. Remember, my daughter, the words of the Divine Master to his apostles, which he directs to us today: "Let not your hearts be troubled" [John 14:1]. Yes, little daughter, do not let your heart be in turmoil in the hour of trial, because Jesus has promised his assistance to whoever follows him.

(To Antonietta Vona, January 2, 1918)

January 2

In order to have a continuously devout life, you need nothing more than to establish a few excellent and noble principles solidly within yourself.

The first principle I want you to understand is from St. Paul: "We know that in everything God works for good with those who love him" [Romans 8:28]. And truly, since God can, and knows how to, bring forth good even from evil, whom will he do this for if not for those who have given themselves completely to him? Perhaps the very sins themselves, which God in his goodness and in his providence is preserving us from committing, are ordained to good for those who serve him. If holy King David had never sinned, he might not have acquired such profound humility. Magdalene would not have loved Jesus so profoundly if he had not forgiven her for many sins....

Meditate, dearest daughter, on this great operation of mercy: It converts our wretchedness into benefits.

(To Antonietta Vona, November 15, 1917)

January 3

The second principle I would like you to have established in your spirit at all times is that God is our Father. What do you have to fear, since you are the daughter of a Father whose providence knows every hair on your head? It is truly a great marvel. Being children of such a Father, how can we have any other thought than loving him and serving him? Be attentive to take care of yourself and your family according to his will, and do not worry about anything else. If you do this, you will see that Jesus is taking care of you. One time he said to St. Catherine of Siena that she should think about him because he was always thinking about her.

(To Antonietta Vona, November 15, 1917)

January 4

The third principle is based on what the Divine Master taught his disciples about not lacking anything.

Pay close attention, my good daughter, to this passage. Jesus had sent his apostles into the world without money, staffs, sandals, and bags and with only one tunic, and then he said to them, "When I sent you out…, did you lack anything?" [Luke 22:35]. And they answered no.

I ask you now, daughter, when you found yourself burdened at a time when you unfortunately did not experience much trust in God, tell me, did you remain oppressed by that trial forever? You will answer no. And so I ask you, why then do you not have the courage to overcome other adversities? If God did not abandon you in the past, why would he ever abandon you in the future?

(To Antonietta Vona, November 15, 1917)

January 5

The fourth principle concerns eternity. These fleeting moments of life should matter little to the sons and daughters of God, because they will live eternally in glory with him. My daughter, remember, you have already begun your journey to eternity; you have already set your foot on that path. Since eternity means happiness for you, what does it matter if some of these passing moments are unpleasant?

The fifth principle that I urge you to keep in mind at all times is from the apostle Paul: "Far be it from me to glory except in the cross of our Lord Jesus Christ" [Galatians 6:14].

Keep the crucified Jesus in your heart, and all the crosses of the world will seem like roses to you. Those who have felt the pricks of the crown of thorns of the Savior, who is our head, will not in any way feel other wounds.

(To Antonietta Vona, November 15, 1917)

January 6

On one occasion I had such an exquisite experience in the most secret and intimate recesses of myself that I do not know how to explain it. My soul felt his presence at first without being able to see him. After that I would say that he came so close to my soul that I literally sensed his touch, so to speak; it was like someone holding another person very tightly.

I do not know what else to say about it, but I confess I was seized by an immense fear at first. However, it soon turned into a heavenly intoxication. I felt as if I were no longer here on earth, and when it happened, I cannot say whether I was still in my body or not. Only God knows, and I cannot say anything more to give you a better idea of what happened.

(To Fr. Benedetto of San Marco in Lamis, March 8, 1916)

January 7

Temptation spares no elect soul. It did not spare the Apostle to the Gentiles, who, after having been taken up into paradise while he was still alive, underwent such a trial that Satan almost succeeded in casting him down. My God! Who can read his writing without feeling the blood run cold in their veins?! How many tears, how many sighs, how many groans, how many prayers did this holy apostle not lift up to the Lord to ask him to remove this very painful trial from him! But how did Jesus answer? "My grace is sufficient for you," and "My power is made perfect in weakness" [2 Corinthians 12:9].

(To Maria Gargani, September 4, 1916)

January 8

Always be strong in your faith, and always be vigilant, so that you can be safe from the snares of the enemy. This is precisely the advice that the prince of the apostles, St. Peter, gives us: "Be sober, be watchful. Your adversary the devil prowls around like a roaring lion, seeking some one to devour. Resist him, firm in your faith" [1 Peter 5:8–9a]. As a great encouragement to all of us, he adds this: "The same experience of suffering is required of your brotherhood throughout the world" [5:9b].

Beloved daughter of Jesus, stir up your faith in the truth of Christian doctrine, especially in the hour of battle, and in particular stir up your faith in the promise of eternal life that our sweetest Lord gives to those who fight with strength and courage. Be strengthened and comforted to know that you are not alone in suffering and that all of the followers of the Nazarene throughout the world suffer the same things.

(To Raffaelina Cerase, November 26, 1914)

January 9

Understanding God's plan for your life should, on the one hand, elicit such gratitude in your heart toward such a good Father that you would lavish continual thanks to your heavenly benefactor.... On the other hand, understanding his plan should strengthen you to refuse to halt your journey because of the pain and sorrow we must endure to reach the end of this very long road.

The Lord told me he revealed these things about his plan to you primarily so that you would not be in doubt about the course of your life. Run the course, then, and do not grow weary.... Run, and may we all run in such a way that, at the end of the journey, we can say with the holy apostle, "I am already on the point of being sacrificed; the time of my departure has come. I have fought the good fight, I have finished the race, I have kept the faith" [2 Timothy 4:6–7].

(To Raffaelina Cerase, November 26, 1914)

January 10

The darkness that surrounds your souls is actually light, but you are correct to say that you can see nothing despite finding yourselves in the middle of a burning bush. The bush burns, the air is full of storm clouds, but you do not see or understand any of it. Nevertheless, God is speaking and is present to the souls that hear, understand, love, and tremble. My daughters, take heart. Do not wait for Tabor to see God. Contemplate him even now on Sinai....

The awareness of your unworthiness and inner defects is a very pure, divine light that is given to you so that you can see what your lives could be—what your potential is to commit any kind of sin—apart from grace.

(To the Ventrella sisters, December 7, 1916)

January 11

This idea of *potential* unworthiness, which consists in knowing what we could be and do without the help of grace, should not be confused with genuine unworthiness.

In the first instance, a self-awareness of one's potential for sin makes a person acceptable and pleasing in the sight of the Most High. Genuine unworthiness, in contrast, is due to the presence of actual iniquity in a person's soul or conscience.

In the darkness in which you find yourselves most of the time, you are not distinguishing between these two kinds of unworthiness. Since you see what you could become, you are now afraid that you already are what is still only *potential* in you.

Not knowing whether you are worthy of love or of hate from God is painful, but it is not a chastisement. People who are or choose to be unworthy never have fear about being unworthy. The kind of uncertainty you are experiencing is allowed by God to happen to every soul, so that no one presumes and becomes careless in the things that concern eternal salvation.

(To the Ventrella sisters, December 7, 1916)

January 12

Remember that if a demon is causing an uproar, it is a sign that he is still on the outside and not on the inside of you. What we need to be terrified about is a demon that is at peace and has harmony with a human soul. Trust me when I speak to you as a brother, with the authority of a priest and as your director: Drive away your vain fears and scatter these shadows that bring the devil closer to you to torment you and make you hang back, even from daily Communion if possible.

I know that the Lord allows these attacks by the enemy because his mercy makes you precious to him, and he wants you to resemble him in his agony in the desert, in the garden, and on the cross. You need to defend yourselves by sending the devil away and scorning his malignant insinuations.

(To the Ventrella sisters, December 7, 1916)

January 13

Be careful not to lose sight of the divine presence in any of your actions. Never undertake any work or activity without first having lifted your mind to God and committing that activity to him with holy intentions. Do the same when you offer thanks for the outcome of all your actions. Always examine whether things unfolded in accord with the right intentions you had at the outset, and if you find anything defective, humbly ask the Lord for forgiveness with a firm resolution to amend your failings.

You must not be disheartened or sink into sadness if your actions do not attain the perfection you intended. What do you expect? We are all fragile, we are earth, and not every plot of land produces the fruit intended by the farmer. Let us always humble ourselves after our failures, recognizing that we are completely helpless without divine assistance.

(To Raffaelina Cerase, December 17, 1914)

January 14

Worrying about an action that did not achieve its pure intention does not constitute humility. It is merely a clear sign that the soul did not place the perfection of an activity in the hands of divine assistance but rather trusted too much in its own strength.

Raffaelina, you will be safe from the hidden schemes of Satan by rejecting his suggestions as soon as they come. May the vigilant grace of the Lord always guard you completely from becoming a prey to that malevolent spirit. It is no small matter for a soul devoted to the Son of God to fall into this terrible monster's wicked snares because of minor shortcomings.

(To Raffaelina Cerase, December 17, 1914)

January 15

Do not immerse yourself in your work and other activities to such a degree that you lose the divine presence. To that purpose, I urge you continually to renew the right intention you had at the beginning and to recite ejaculatory prayers from time to time. Those prayers are like arrows that wound God's heart and oblige him—and this word is not at all exaggerated in this case—oblige him, I tell you, to grant you his graces and his help in everything.

…When you sit down to eat, prayerfully reflect that you have in your midst the divine Master and his holy apostles at the last meal he had with them when he instituted the sacrament of the altar.

(To Raffaelina Cerase, December 17, 1914)

January 16

In a word, let us try to make our meals be a preparation for the divine meal of the most holy Eucharist.

…Do not eat more food than you need, and try to have moderation in all things. Most of all, determine in your heart to be disposed toward less rather than more at meals. I do not mean, however, that you should leave the table fasting. No, that is not what I mean. Let everything be done prudently, which is the rule for all human actions.

Do not go to bed without having first examined your conscience about what happened during the day and directing all your thoughts to God. Then offer and consecrate yourself and all Christians to him— especially me, a lowly brother who does the same for you.

In addition, offer your sleep to the glory of God's divine majesty, and do not forget the guardian angel who is always with you and never leaves you, no matter what wrong thing you might do.

(To Raffaelina Cerase, December 17, 1914)

January 17

My brother, if being able to stand depended on us, we would all certainly fall into the hands of the enemy of our salvation at the very first gust of wind. Let us always trust in divine mercy, and we will always increasingly experience how good the Lord is....

I urge you earnestly not to spend time thinking about the past. If your time was well used, then let us give God glory. If it was wasted, let us despise it and trust in the goodness of the heavenly Father. Therefore I exhort you to set your mind at rest with the consoling thought that any part of your life that was not well spent has already been forgiven by our most tender God.

Avoid anxieties and worry with all your might. Otherwise, all your activities will have little success or be unfruitful. We know for certain that if our spirits are in turmoil, the attacks of the devil will become more frequent and direct. He always takes advantage of our weaknesses to achieve his intentions.

(To Fr. Basilio of Mirabello Sannitico, February 9, 1916)

January 18

My daughter, do not fear harsh winter storms, because to the extent that winter is harsh, so much more will the spring be full of flowers and the harvest more abundant. Whatever the tempter says or does, God is accomplishing his wonderful purpose for you, which is to complete your full transformation in him. My dearest daughter, do not believe the malignant whisperings and shadows of the enemy. Hold firm the truth of what I declare to you with a clear conscience in my authority as your spiritual director. Being afraid of casting yourself into the arms of divine goodness is even stranger than a baby being afraid while it is held tightly in its mother's arms. Banish whatever doubts or anxieties you have, even though infinite charity can permit them for the same reason I mentioned above.

(To Antonietta Vona, May 21, 1918)

January 19

Be patient, my daughter, in putting up with your imperfections if you wish to attain perfection.

Remember, this is a very important point if we want to make progress on the paths that lead us to God. When you cannot make great strides on your path, be content with small steps, waiting patiently for legs to run or, even better, wings to fly. Be content for now, my daughter, to be a small bee in the honeycomb, for very soon you will become a large bee capable of producing honey.

Humble yourself lovingly before God and before others, because God speaks to the lowly. "Hear," he says to the bride in the holy psalms, "consider, and incline your ear; forget your people and your father's house" [Psalm 45:10]. This is the attitude with which a loving child lies prostrate when speaking to the heavenly Father and waits for his divine answer.

God will fill your vase with his balm when he sees it is empty of the world's perfumes. And the more he humbles you, the more he will exalt you.

(To Antonietta Vona, May 21, 1918)

January 20

I find it absolutely impossible to explain the workings of love. Infinite love has finally conquered the hardness of my heart through its immense power, and I find myself annihilated and reduced to helplessness.

He has been pouring himself completely into the small vessel of the creature I am. I am suffering an unspeakable martyrdom and feel myself incapable of carrying the weight of this immense love. Oh! Who will come to relieve me? How will I be able to carry the infinite in such a small heart? How will I ever be able to contain the infinite inside the small, narrow room of my soul?

(To Fr. Benedetto of San Marco in Lamis, January 12, 1919)

January 21

My soul is melting with sorrow and love, with bitterness and sweetness, at the same time. How will I bear up under such an overwhelming action of the Most High? I possess him now, and my jubilation compels me to say with the Blessed Virgin, "My spirit rejoices in God my Savior" [Luke 1:47].

I possess him inside myself, and I feel all the intensity of repeating what the bride in the Song of Solomon says: "I found him whom my soul loves. I held him, and would not let him go" [3:4]. But when I feel I am unable to bear the weight of this infinite love and have to contain it in the smallness of my being, I become filled with terror that perhaps I will lose him because I will not succeed in containing him in the narrow little cell of my heart.

(To Fr. Benedetto of San Marco in Lamis, January 12, 1919)

January 22

Father, I cannot survive this pain. In trying to hold up under it, I feel myself crushed and my life slipping away. I cannot tell you if I am alive or not in those moments. I am outside of myself. Pain and sweetness clash within me, and my soul experiences a swoon that is both sweet and bitter.

The embraces of delight follow one another in abundance (and I would say relentlessly and without measure). My efforts to prop myself up do not succeed in preventing the acute martyrdom of feeling incapable of bearing the weight of an infinite love.

(To Fr. Benedetto of San Marco in Lamis, January 12, 1919)

January 23

Why are we alive? After our consecration through baptism, we belong to Jesus Christ. Therefore every Christian soul should be familiar with the saying of the holy apostle, "To me to live is Christ" [Philippians 1:21]. I live through Jesus Christ, I live for his glory, I live to serve him, I live to love him. When God brings our lives to an end, the sentiment or feeling that we should have is exactly the feeling of someone who receives a reward after working hard or a crown after battle.

Let us cherish, yes, cherish, my dear Raffaelina, this apostle's lofty disposition of soul.... Let us always dispose ourselves to recognize the very wise ordering of Divine Providence in all the events of life. Let us adore him and dispose our wills always and in all things to be conformed to God's will.

(To Raffaelina Cerase, February 23, 1915)

January 24

The apostle rejoices at the thought that he will not be ashamed of anything and will not in any way neglect his duty as an apostle of Jesus Christ. He rejoices, even in the midst of the chains of his imprisonment, that Jesus will always be exalted in his body. If he lives, he will exalt Jesus Christ through his life and his preaching, even while he is in prison. He had always preached until that time, and now he preaches to the praetorian guard. If he will be martyred, then he will glorify Jesus Christ by offering the supreme testimony of his love.

Thus he declares openly that for him his life is Christ, who is the heart and center of his entire life, the motive for all his actions, the ultimate goal of all his aspirations. Paul then adds that death would be a gain for him, because through his martyrdom he would give solemn testimony to Jesus by his love. It would make his union with Jesus even more indissoluble and would increase the glory that awaits him.

(To Raffaelina Cerase, February 23, 1915)

January 25

Both these attitudes in St. Paul proceed from perfect love. His desire to depart from this life means he would be in perfect union with Jesus Christ in glory, and that would be better for him, that is, it would be more desirable than continuing to live on this earth. This desire is grounded in the perfect charity he has toward God. The other desire also proceeds from perfect charity, but its immediate goal is the salvation of his neighbor. This second desire, then, is motivated by his principal goal, God, but its outworking is expressed in relation to the salvation of souls.

Leaving his body is more beneficial to him, and he desires that as ardently as any righteous soul desires to be united to God. As for continuing to remain on earth in the midst of toil and trouble for the salvation of souls, being full of the spirit of Jesus Christ he sees that his staying would be more beneficial for others.

(To Raffaelina Cerase, February 23, 1915)

January 26

This grace [of seeing the Lord] has produced much good in me. My soul is constantly in great peace. I feel myself strongly consumed by an extraordinarily enormous desire to please God. Ever since the Lord favored me with this grace, I have viewed with immense disdain everything that does not help me come closer to God. I feel an unspeakable embarrassment at not being able to understand why such a great blessing was ever given to me.

My soul is stirred by my sincerest gratitude to testify to the Lord that this grace he is giving me is not due to any merit of my own, so for that reason I can hardly believe myself superior to other people. On the contrary, I believe that out of so many people in the world this grace is given to the one who is the least useful to the Lord. The Lord has brought me such clarity through this grace that I realize I am now obliged to serve and love him more than any other person.

(To Fr. Benedetto in San Marco in Lamis, July 7, 1913)

January 27

Providence has led us away from ignoring the soul and from making only our bodies beautiful. In his infinite wisdom, God has in fact placed in our hands all the means necessary to make our souls beautiful, even after we deform them by sin. It is sufficient that a soul wishes to cooperate with divine grace in order for its beauty to attain such splendor, such loveliness, such gracefulness, that it can draw to itself, through love and amazement, not so much the eyes of the angels but the very eyes of God, according to the testimony of sacred Scripture: "The King (meaning God) will desire your beauty" [Psalm 45:11].

(To Raffaelina Cerase, November 16, 1914)

January 28

My daughter, let us understand and be resigned to this great and terrible truth: Self-love will never die before we do. The sad truth that we have inherited the guilt of original sin as a punishment certainly grieves us. Nevertheless, we need to resign ourselves and have patience with ourselves, since, as the divine teaching says, by patience we will gain our souls. This self-possession will be much firmer when it is less assailed by cares and anxieties—even anxieties about our imperfections.

We will always experience the palpable attacks and the secret workings of self-love, until we leave this earth. To avoid offending God and disfiguring our souls, it is enough that we do not deliberately consent to it by our will....

Come, my daughter, be at peace. If you violate the principle of detachment by spontaneous impulses of self-love or passion concerning things that should be treated with indifference, just prostrate yourself as soon as you can, and lift your heart to God. Say to him in a confident and humble spirit, "Lord, have mercy on me, because I am only a weakling." Then rise up in peace and, with a serene, tranquil heart and holy detachment, go about your business.

(To Maria Gargani, February 12, 1917)

January 29

Always keep in mind that the people of Israel spent forty years in the desert before reaching the Promised Land, even though the journey should not have taken more than six weeks. They were not permitted to ask why God led them in circuitous and arduous ways, and all those who complained about it died before reaching their destination. Even Moses, that great friend of God, died on the border of the Promised Land and saw it only from afar, without being able to enjoy it himself. Do not focus so much on the path you have; keep your eyes fixed instead on the one who guides you and on the heavenly home to which he is guiding you. Why should you care if you are walking through the desert or through meadows, provided that God is always with you and you succeed in possessing blessed eternity?

(To Antonietta Vona, December 6, 1917)

January 30

My son, why are you so full of anxiety about your soul? Why do you consider yourself full of wretchedness and weakness? Look, this situation is just another opportunity for you to be about the business of tending to your soul; it can be another source of merit for you. Humble yourself before the good Lord, and continue to ask him to free you from that state of wretchedness and weakness. Ardently desire to be free of that state and, for your part, do not neglect what you know you need to do in order to recover.

Meanwhile, be patient in enduring your shortcomings if you want to be perfect. This is a very significant point for any soul that aims for perfection. "By your endurance," says the divine Master, "you will gain your lives" [Luke 21:19]. Therefore be patient with yourself and your weaknesses, and in the meantime do your best to use the means that you already knew about and the ones you have learned from me and from others.

(To Br. Marcellino Diconsole, January 30, 1919)

January 31

I have told you many times that in spiritual life you need to walk by faith…. Go about it this way: Insofar as your ability and your weakness allow, aim to do good at all times. If you succeed in doing that, praise and thank God. If, despite your vigilance and goodwill, you do not succeed in doing good either in part or altogether, humble yourself profoundly before God but without discouragement. Determine to be more careful in the future, ask for divine assistance, and move forward.

I know that you do not deliberately wish to do evil. The evils that the Lord permits and that happen without your wanting them serve to humble you and to keep you free from self-conceit. Do not be afraid, therefore, and do not be anxious any longer about doubts of conscience, because you know full well that, after being diligent and having done what you could, there is no more room for fear and worry.

(To Br. Marcellino Diconsole, January 30, 1919)

FEBRUARY

February 1

Always humble yourself before the mercy of our God, and thank him for the favors he has shown you. This is the best disposition from which to receive new graces that our heavenly Father, out of the depth of his love for you, wants to give you. It is only logical that a person who does not respond with gratitude and continual thanksgiving for such gifts does not deserve to receive more of them.

Yes, entrust yourself to God and always thank him for everything, and you will defy and conquer all the wrath of hell.

(To Raffaelina Cerase, April 20, 1915)

February 2

Listen to the just complaints of our very sweet Jesus: "My love is repaid with so much ingratitude! I would be less offended by people if I had loved them less. My Father no longer wants to endure this from them. I would like to stop loving them, but…" (And here Jesus becomes silent and sighs.) "But oh! My heart is made to love! Weak and cowardly men put forth no concerted effort to overcome temptations and even delight in their iniquities. When my most beloved souls are put to the test, they come to me less often. The weak abandon themselves to despair and dismay, and the strong gradually slacken their efforts.

"They leave me alone at night and alone in churches during the day. They no longer care about the Eucharist. People never speak about this sacrament of love, and those that do speak about it do so with indifference and coldness.

"My heart has been forgotten. No one cares about my love anymore, and I am always saddened by that. My house has become a theater of entertainment for many. The ministers whom I have always regarded with favor and have loved as the apple of my eye should comfort my heart, which is overflowing with sorrow. They should help me in the redemption of souls. Instead—who would believe it!—they treat me with ingratitude and neglect."

Jesus continued his lament. Father, how it pains me to see Jesus weep! Have you had that experience too?

(To Fr. Agostino of San Marco in Lamis, March 12, 1913)

February 3

You can be sure that the trials you are going through are all clear signs of divine delight and jewels to beautify your soul. Everything that is happening in you is the work of Jesus, and you need to believe that. It is not your place to monitor the Lord's work but instead to submit humbly to his divine operations. Give full freedom to the grace that is at work in you. Remember never to become distressed by any adverse thing that happens, knowing that distress is an impediment to the Holy Spirit.

Therefore, whenever you sense some uneasiness arising, run to God and abandon yourself to him with complete childlike trust, because it is written that whoever trusts in him will not be put to shame [see Isaiah 49:23b]. Always be courageous and move forward. Winter will pass, and unending spring will come with abundant goodness that far outweighs the harshness of the storms.

The dryness of spirit that disturbs you is a very painful trial, but it is a very wonderful thing because of its spiritual fruit…. God ordains this kind of dryness to help the soul attain true devotion, which consists in a prompt willingness to serve God without any personal reward. In brief, do good insofar as it is good in itself and insofar as it gives glory and pleasure to God.

(To Maria Gargani, August 26, 1916)

February 4

You know how it pains me to see so many pitiful blind people fleeing hurriedly from this very gracious offer of the Master, "If any one thirst, let him come to me and drink" [John 7:37].

My soul is extremely distressed when I see these truly blind people who do not feel even a bit of mercy for themselves, whose passions have robbed them of wisdom, and who do not even think about coming to drink the genuine water of paradise.

Take a look, my father, and tell me if I am right to be unhappy about the folly of these blind people. Look at how the enemies of the cross triumph more every day. Oh heaven! They are constantly on fire with thousands of desires for earthly satisfactions....

Jesus extends his very tender invitation to come and drink the living water, but oh God! What response does he get from these wretched people? They pretend not to understand, they flee, and, what is worse, after a long time these miserable people become accustomed to living in that fire for earthly satisfactions and grow older in the midst of those flames.

(To Fr. Agostino of San Marco in Lamis, October 10, 1915)

February 5

What medicine is there to make these wretched Judases come to their senses? What medicine can we hope will bring these people who are truly dead back to life? Oh, my father, my soul is bursting with sorrow. Jesus gave a welcome, an embrace, a kiss to them as well. But for these wretched people it was a welcome that has not sanctified them, an embrace that has not converted them, and a kiss, unfortunately, that not only has not saved them but may perhaps never even save a large majority of them! Divine mercy no longer softens them; his blessings do not draw them. His punishments do not tame them with sweetness. When he treats them kindly, they become insolent, and when he is stern, they rage severely against him. In prosperity they gloat; in adversity they become dejected. They are deaf, blind, and insensitive to every sweet invitation and every severe reproof of divine mercy that could awaken and convert them. They only harden themselves in their condition and make their darkness more intense.

(To Fr. Agostino of San Marco in Lamis, October 10, 1915)

February 6

May it please the Lord, the source of all life, not to withhold from me that sweet, precious water he promised out of his overflowing love to whosoever thirsts. I long for this water, my father. I beg Jesus for it with continuous sighs and groans. Please pray that he not hold it back from me. Tell him, my father, that he knows how much I need this water, which alone can heal my soul that has been wounded by love.

May this most tender Bridegroom of the Song of Solomon comfort my soul, which thirsts for him, with the same divine kiss the bride was seeking from him. Tell him that until my soul receives that kiss, I will not be able to make a covenant with him and say, "I am my beloved's and my beloved is mine" [Song of Solomon 6:3].

(To Fr. Agostino of San Marco in Lamis, October 10, 1915)

February 7

If you are to reciprocate [God's love for you] generously, make yourself worthy of him, that is, be like him in his divine perfections that you have already learned about in the Scripture and the Gospels. However, for you to imitate him, my brother, you need to reflect and meditate on his life regularly. Continual reflection and meditation will make you esteem his actions, and that will bring forth the desire and motivation for imitation. This is already incorporated into the rules of our order, so let us be faithful to their exact observance, and we will attain perfection.

Primarily you need to focus on the foundation of Christian righteousness and goodness, that is, the virtue our Master and our seraphic father [St. Francis] modeled for us: humility.

(To Br. Gerardo Deliceto, August 19, 1918)

February 8

We are capable of turning good into evil, of abandoning the good for evil, of attributing to ourselves good that we do not have or that has been loaned to us, of justifying our wrongdoing, and, in coddling our wrongdoing, of scorning the Highest Good.

With this clearly understood,

1. You must *never* flatter yourself for whatever good you might notice in yourself, because everything good comes to you from God, and you need to give the honor and glory to him.

2. Do not complain about offenses done to you, no matter where they come from.

3. You must forgive everyone with Christian charity, remembering the example of the Redeemer, who forgave even those who crucified him....

4. You must *always* humble yourself before God because of your spiritual poverty.

5. You must not be surprised *at all* at your weaknesses and imperfections, but, recognizing who you are, you need to blush at your inconstancy and unfaithfulness to God.

(To Br. Gerardo Deliceto, August 19, 1918)

February 9

You can be certain, my dear, that what most assures us of perfection is the virtue of patience. If it is necessary to practice it with other people, then it is indeed fitting that we exercise it toward ourselves as well. In fact, people who aspire to a pure love for God need more patience with themselves than with others. We need to resign ourselves, my dear daughter, to enduring our imperfections so that we can arrive at perfection. I am saying that you should put up with imperfections—that does not mean you should cherish them or be fond of them—because humility grows through this suffering.

(To Erminia Gargani, March 3, 1917)

February 10

It is time for us to admit it: We are pitiable because we are rarely able to practice doing good. But God in his goodness pities us and contents himself with the little we do. He accepts the preparations of our hearts. What is the preparation of our hearts?...We prepare our hearts when we set ourselves aside to meditate and dispose ourselves for the service we owe to God of loving him, loving our neighbor, mortifying our external and internal senses, and practicing other good spiritual exercises.

As we do this, our hearts become prepared and thus dispose our actions to a preeminent degree of Christian perfection. However, my dear daughter, none of this is proportional to the greatness of God, who is infinitely greater than the whole universe, our strength, and our actions. Anyone who does consider God's grandeur, his goodness, and his immense glory cannot hold back from making great preparations for him.

(To Erminia Gargani, March 3, 1917)

February 11

Do we want to proceed in a good fashion? Then let us focus on walking the path that is closest to us. Remember well what I am about to tell you.... Our imperfection will accompany us right to the grave. We will not get there without being part earth. Nevertheless, it is not acceptable to become sleepy or to turn back just because we are like small chicks without wings. We are dying little by little in our physical lives, and that is an ordinary law of providence. Similarly, we need to make our imperfections die day by day as well. We could exclaim, "Oh happy imperfections!" because they make us aware of our great poverty. They train us to be humble, to deny ourselves, to be patient, and to be diligent. Despite our imperfections, God looks on the preparations of our hearts.

(To Erminia Gargani, March 3, 1917)

February 12

Let us stay at the divine Master's feet with Magdalene. Practice the virtues that are appropriate for you: patience, tolerance of your neighbors, humility, gentleness, friendliness, suffering because of your imperfections, and many others.

I recommend holy simplicity to you, a virtue that is very close to my heart. Always look straight ahead without wracking your brain, thinking about the dangers you see far off.... Do not pay attention to them; otherwise you could make some false steps as you go forward. Always have a firm and determined intention of wanting to serve God with all your heart for your whole life. Do not be concerned about tomorrow, and think only about doing good today. When tomorrow comes and is called "today," then you can think about it.

(To Erminia Gargani, March 3, 1917)

February 13

You need to have great trust in Divine Providence even to be able to practice holy simplicity. My daughter, you need to imitate the people of God when they found themselves in the desert: They were expressly forbidden from gathering more manna than they needed for a day. Well, we too need the provisions of manna only for one day. Have no doubts, my daughter, that God will provide for tomorrow and for all the remaining days of our journey.

(To Erminia Gargani, March 3, 1917)

February 14

Imitate Jesus in his charity, because he recognizes as his own only those who jealously guard this precious flower. Remember that all of God's judgment—when we come into his divine presence—will center on this virtue of charity….Yes, evaluate all your actions by the standard of love, and you will be weaving for yourselves a crown of merit in heaven.

You should not let any difficulties you experience in practicing virtue or in praying disturb you or make you hold back from practicing either of those activities, so continue in your practice of them. Do not consider it a waste of time whenever you need to do them out of sheer obedience.

(To Franciscan novices, January 7, 1919)

February 15

Jesus tells me that when it comes to love, he is the one who delights in me; when it comes to sorrow, instead it is I who delight in him. For me to desire health right now would be seeking joy for myself and not seeking to comfort Jesus. Yes, I love the cross and only the cross. I love it because I always see it on Jesus' shoulders. By now Jesus knows full well that my whole life, my whole heart, is dedicated to him and to his sufferings.

Oh father! Forgive me for using such language. Only Jesus can comprehend the pain there is for me when I place myself before the sorrowful scene of Calvary. It is incomprehensible that Jesus is comforted not only by sharing his sorrows but also by finding a soul who, out of love for him, asks not for consolation but for participation in his very sufferings.

When Jesus wants me to know he loves me, he lets me experience his wounds, his thorns, his agonies.

(To Fr. Agostino of San Marco in Lamis, February 1, 1913)

February 16

Take comfort because your suffering is in God's will. If human nature is resentful of suffering and resists it…, that is because human beings were created for happiness, and crosses are a consequence of sin. As long as we are on this earth, we will always feel a natural aversion to suffering. It is a chain that accompanies us everywhere we go. You can be certain, however, that even if our disposition is to desire the cross and we willingly embrace it and submit to it out of love for God, that does not mean we will stop feeling nature's demands in our flesh to not want to suffer. Who most loved the cross of the divine Master? Well, even he, in his most holy humanity during his freely chosen agony, prayed that the chalice be removed from him if possible.

(To Raffaelina Cerase, May 13, 1915)

February 17

Baptism is said to be a copy of the death of Jesus. St. Paul says we are baptized "into his death" [Romans 6:3], in imitation of the death of our Redeemer. What the cross was to Jesus, then, baptism is for us. Jesus Christ was nailed to the cross to die in his flesh. We are baptized to die to sin, to die to ourselves. On the cross Jesus Christ had all his senses put to death, so we through baptism should carry the death of Jesus in all our senses. This is precisely what St. Paul says in his second letter to the faithful in Corinth: "[We are] always carrying in the body the death of Jesus, so that the life of Jesus may also be manifested in our bodies" [2 Corinthians 4:10].

(To Raffaelina Cerase, September 19, 1914)

February 18

Through baptism a Christian receives new life in Christ, becomes lifted up into a supernatural life, and acquires the wonderful hope of being seated on a heavenly throne in glory. What dignity! The Christian vocation involves a continual aspiration to the homeland of the blessed. The Christian vocation requires us, I tell you, not to set our hearts on the things of this vile world. All the concern and effort of a good Christian who is living out this vocation is focused on obtaining eternal benefits. The Christian needs to judge things here below by esteeming and valuing only those things that are helpful in obtaining eternal benefits and dismissing all the things that are not helpful in reaching that goal.

(To Raffaelina Cerase, November 16, 1914)

February 19

Always live your life far away from the corruption of the worldly Jerusalem, unholy assemblies, corrupt entertainment that is itself corrupting, and any fellowship with wicked people.

Be ready, like the holy Redeemer was, to drink with him the dark water of the Kidron River, accepting tribulation and penance with devout resignation. Cross over the Kidron with Jesus, suffering the disdain of the world with constancy and courage out of love for Jesus. Always keep yourself recollected, and let your life be hidden in Jesus and with him in the Garden of Gethsemane, that is, in the silence of meditation and solitude, so that the flood of humiliations do not block your journey. Go forward, always go forward, Raffaelina, and do not let the bitterness of the river of humiliation hold you back. Do not let persecution by worldly people and those who do not live in the spirit of Jesus Christ lead you away from walking on the path the saints walked. Always run toward the steep slope of the mountain of holiness, and do not be dismayed by the arduous path.

(To Raffaelina Cerase, August 4, 1915)

February 20

Jesus, the man of sorrows, would like all Christians to imitate him. Jesus has now offered me the chalice again. I accepted it, and this is why he does not spare me from it:

My paltry suffering is worth nothing, but in fact it pleases Jesus.... Consequently, on certain special days during which he suffered greatly on this earth, he makes me feel his suffering even more intensely.

I have been made worthy to suffer with Jesus and like Jesus. Shouldn't this be enough to humble me and cause me to try to hide myself from people's eyes?

Oh my father, the ingratitude toward the majesty of God that I feel within me is so immense.

(To Fr. Agostino of San Marco in Lamis, February 1, 1913)

February 21

Consider Jesus' *fiat* in the garden ["Not my will, but yours, be done" (Luke 22:42)]. What a weight he must have felt to have sweat, and to have sweat blood! Proclaim your *fiat* too, as much in propitious times as in adverse circumstances. Do not worry or wrestle with how you will be able to express it. We know that human nature avoids difficult things, like the cross, but that does not mean the soul is not submitted to God's will once it is understood....

Would you like me to give you proof that a will has proclaimed its *fiat*? Virtue is known by its opposite, so tell me, in a difficult or easy trial, do you feel yourself rebelling against God? Better yet, let's take an outrageous example: Try hard to rebel. Now, tell me, weren't you horrified at the very sound of this blasphemous idea? Well, there is no intermediate response between yes and no here.

If your will recoils from the idea of rebellion, then be assured it is tacitly or explicitly submitted to God's will. Consequently, be assured that your will is proclaiming its *fiat* in some way.

(To Raffaelina Cerase, January 30, 1915)

February 22

St. Paul tells us that "those who belong to Christ Jesus have crucified the flesh with its passions and desires" [Galatians 5:24]. It seems from this teaching that whoever wants to be a true Christian, that is, one who lives in the spirit of Jesus Christ, must mortify the flesh for no other reason than devotion to Jesus—who for love of us chose to mortify his limbs on the cross. Mortification must be steady, ongoing, and consistent, and it must last throughout our lives. The perfect Christian must not be content with mortification that is severe only in appearance; it should actually be painful.

Since this is how mortification occurs, the apostle rightly calls it a crucifixion....You need to dominate the flesh, to crucify it, because the flesh is at the root of all evils.

(To Raffaelina Cerase, October 23, 1914)

February 23

Vainglory, or self-conceit, is the true enemy of souls who are consecrated to the Lord and are committed to spiritual life. That is precisely why it can be said to be the devouring worm of any soul that aims for perfection. The saints have called it the worm that destroys holiness.

To demonstrate how self-conceit is the opposite of perfection, Our Lord rebuked the apostles when he saw they were full of self-satisfaction and vainglory after they saw that demons obeyed their commands: "Nevertheless do not rejoice in this, that the spirits are subject to you" [Luke 10:20].

To uproot the evil effects of that accursed vice from their minds, lest it succeed in insinuating itself into their hearts, he terrified them by giving them the example of Lucifer falling from the heights to which God had raised him, falling because of self-conceit based on the gifts he had received: "I saw Satan fall like lightning from heaven" [Luke 10:18].

This vice is even more to be feared because there is no opposing virtue to counter it. Every vice actually has its remedy in an opposite virtue. Anger is overcome through meekness, envy through charity, pride through humility, and so on. Only the vice of self-conceit does not have a contrary virtue to counteract it. It insinuates itself into the holiest of actions, and, if it is not recognized, it haughtily sets up its tent even in humility.

(To Fr. Agostino of San Marco in Lamis, August 2, 1913)

February 24

The devil, dear father, knows well that a lewd person, a predator, a greedy person, a sinner, has more to be embarrassed and blush about than to boast about, so he avoids tempting them with self-conceit. Although he spares them that battle, he does not spare good people, most especially those who are aiming at perfection. Other vices prevail over only those who let themselves be overcome and dominated by them. However, self-conceit raises its head against the very people who fight and overcome it. Conceit goes forth to wage war against these conquerors, to remove the very victories that they have won. It is an enemy that never grows weary and wars against us in all our actions. If we are not aware of its presence, we become its victims.

In fact, to flee the praises of others, we prefer hidden fasts to those in the open, silence rather than eloquent speech, being scorned rather than being considered important, contempt rather than honor. Alas, my God, even when we do these things, self-conceit wants to poke its nose in, as they say, and attacks us with self-satisfaction.

(To Fr. Agostino of San Marco in Lamis, August 2, 1913)

February 25

St. Jerome was right to compare self-conceit to a shadow, because a shadow follows the body wherever it goes and imitates its movements. When the body flees, it flees too. If someone walks with slow steps, it conforms to those steps. If a person sits, the shadow takes that same posture.

Similarly, self-conceit follows virtue everywhere. The body would flee its own shadow in vain, because the shadow always and everywhere follows the body and pursues it. In a similar way, this happens to whoever aims for virtue and perfection. The more one attempts to flee self-satisfaction, the more closely it follows....

Let us always be on the alert and not let this very formidable enemy penetrate our minds and hearts, because, once it enters, it ravages every virtue, mars every holiness, and corrupts everything that is good and beautiful.

(To Fr. Agostino of San Marco in Lamis, August 2, 1913)

February 26

Let us always seek to ask God for the grace to be preserved from this pestilent vice [of self-conceit], because "every perfect gift is from above, coming down from the Father of lights" [James 1:17].... Let us always remember that everything that is good in us is a pure gift from the supreme goodness of the heavenly Bridegroom.

Let us imprint this on our minds, engrave it deeply in our hearts, and be fully persuaded about it: "No one is good but God alone" [Mark 10:18]; we are and have nothing in ourselves. Let us meditate constantly on what St. Paul wrote to the faithful in Corinth: "What have you that you did not receive? If then you received it, why do you boast as if it were not a gift?" [1 Corinthians 4:7].

...If the enemy assails our paths because of the holiness of our lives, we should shout to his face, "My holiness does not come from my spirit but comes rather from the Spirit of God who sanctifies me. It is a gift of God. It is like a talent loaned to me by my Bridegroom so that I can do business with it and then render a strict account of the gains I have made through it."

(To Fr. Agostino of San Marco in Lamis, August 2, 1913)

February 27

Virtues are like treasures that will get stolen if they are not hidden from the eyes of the envious. The devil is always vigilant, and he is the worst of all those who envy, because he quickly tries to steal these treasures—our virtues—when he is presumably out of sight, and he does it by attacking us through the very formidable enemy of self-conceit.

Our Lord, who is always solicitous of our good, warns us about it in various places in the gospel in order to preserve us from this great enemy. Does he not tell us when we want to pray that we should withdraw to our room and close the door as we pray face-to-face with God, so that our prayers are not seen by others? That when fasting we should wash our faces, so that others do not know we are fasting because of our pale faces? That in giving alms we should not let the right hand know what the left hand is doing?

(To Fr. Agostino of San Marco in Lamis, August 2, 1913)

February 28

St. Paul experienced the rebellion of the senses and passions rather intensely, which made him cry out, "I of myself serve the law of God with my mind, but with my flesh I serve the law of sin" [Romans 7:25], that is, the law of concupiscence….

This is a comfort for so many souls who experience this sharp conflict within themselves. They do not want to have impulses of rancor or vivid fantasies or sensual feelings, and they are hindered by these things that rise up against their will. They feel a strong propensity within themselves toward evil when doing the very action they had intended for good.

Some of these poor souls believe they are offending the Lord by experiencing this propensity. Be comforted, elect souls, in the fact that there is no sin in this, because the holy apostle himself, the chosen vessel, experienced this horrible inner conflict too: "I do not do the good I want, but the evil I do not want is what I do" [Romans 7:19]. Feeling the urgings of the flesh in such a way does not constitute sin when the soul has not freely chosen them.

(To Raffaelina Cerase, November 16, 1914)

February 29

To worldly people it seems impossible to believe that there are souls who suffer because providence is prolonging their lives....

Seeing the intense pain the souls of the righteous suffer on earth in being away from the Lord, their center, we can form a dim idea, Raffaelina, of what those souls suffer in the very duty of satisfying the basic needs of life—eating, drinking, sleeping.... I can truly compare that suffering only to the suffering of martyrs who were burned alive and gave their lives to Jesus in that way as a testimony of their faith.

Some people might think that comparing them to martyrs is an exaggeration, pure and simple, but I know, my dear Raffaelina, what I am talking about. On the day of universal judgment, I assure you that we will see these souls who, without spilling their blood for the faith, will be crowned like martyrs and given martyrs' palms.

(To Raffaelina Cerase, February 23, 1915)

MARCH

March 1

Dearest father,

I would like to reveal my heart to you for just a moment, so that you can see the wound that our sweetest Jesus has lovingly opened in my heart!…

You already know this Lover who never gets angry with whoever offends him. The One I carry in my heart is infinitely merciful. My heart knows it has nothing to boast about in front of him. He has loved me and chosen to favor me above so many others.

When I ask what I have done to merit so many consolations, he smiles and…asks only my love in return, but do I not owe that to him already out of sheer gratitude?

Oh my father, if I could only make him happy just a little in the way that he makes me so happy!… My father, if Jesus can make us so happy on earth, what will it be like in heaven?

(To Fr. Agostino of San Marco in Lamis, December 3, 1912)

March 2

Every small thing I do wrong is a painful sword that pierces my heart. At certain times I am led to exclaim with the apostle, but not with his perfection, "It is no longer I who live, but Christ who lives in me" [Galatians 2:20], because I do sense someone living in me.

The other result of this grace is that life has become a cruel martyrdom for me, and I am comforted only by resigning myself to continue living on earth because of my love for Jesus. However, my father, even with that comfort, the pain I feel at certain times is unbearable....

Before the Lord favored me with this grace, neither sorrow for my sins, nor the pain I felt when I offended the Lord, nor the fullness of the affection I felt for God was strong enough to make me leave my whole self behind. When at times that situation seemed unbearable to me, I was forced to express myself with very bitter cries that I could not hold back. But since this grace was given, the pain has become even more intense, and now it seems to me that my heart is pierced on all sides.

(To Fr. Benedetto of San Marco in Lamis, July 7, 1913)

March 3

People should be careful not to speak with others, apart from their spiritual directors, about the favors the Lord is bestowing on them. They ought always to direct their actions to the pure glory of God, which is what the apostle counsels: "Whether you eat or drink or whatever you do, do all to the glory of God" [1 Corinthians 10:31]. This holy resolve needs to be renewed from time to time. If we examine our actions and see some imperfections, we should not be dismayed. We should abase and humble ourselves before God's goodness, ask for forgiveness, and beg him to guard us from that in the future.

(To Fr. Agostino of San Marco in Lamis, August 2, 1913)

March 4

Any mental picture of your life that focuses on past sins is a lie and thus comes from the devil. Jesus loves you and has forgiven you your sins, so there is no room for having a downcast spirit. Whatever persuades you otherwise is truly a waste of time. It is also something that offends the heart of our very tender Lover. On the other hand, if the mental picture of your life consists in what you can be or could be, then it comes from God.

Your impulse to be in a peaceful cloister is holy, but it needs to be qualified. It is better to do God's will by waiting a little longer outside the sacred enclosure, if that is what charity demands, than to enjoy the refreshing shade of the sacred cloister.

(To Maria Gargani, August 26, 1916)

March 5

Beloved father, I urge you to calm your worries about your spirit, because they seem to me to be a true waste of time in relation to eternity. What is worse is that...your good deeds could become sullied, if you will allow me to use that word, by some lack of trust in God's goodness....

...That is a serious injustice the soul does to our heavenly Bridegroom and in consequence, alas! we are deprived of so many graces by our sweetest Lord precisely because the door of our heart is not open to him with holy confidence. If a soul does not resolve to come out of that state, it draws many chastisements to itself.

Do not think my assertion is exaggerated, dear father. Let us remember the immense number of God's people in the desert who did not set foot in the Promised Land through a lack of trust. Even their own leader, Moses, who hesitated as he struck the rock [in anger] for water to quench the people's thirst, was severely punished and did not enter the Promised Land.

(To Fr. Agostino of San Marco in Lamis, August 17, 1913)

March 6

I am experiencing a very strong desire—without, however, attaining it most of the time—to live every moment of my life loving the Lord. I want to keep myself very close to him and hold his hand as I joyfully walk the sorrowful path on which he has placed me. But I say, with a heavy heart, with consternation in my soul, and with shame on my face, my desires do not in fact correspond to the reality.

It takes only the least little thing for me to get agitated. All I have to do is forget your reassurances to me and I am flinging myself into the darkest spiritual confusion that makes me suffer terribly day and night....

I want to think only about Jesus. I want my heart to beat only and always for him, and I have promised all this to Jesus in earnest. But alas! I realize only too well that my mind wanders or even ceases to function in a difficult spiritual trial, and then my heart can do nothing except languish in that sorrow.

(To Fr. Benedetto of San Marco in Lamis, March 6, 1917)

March 7

It is true that I have consecrated everything to Jesus and intend to suffer everything for his sake. But I am not convinced this is really the case. I am completely deprived of light, and that is enough to fill me with fear and dread and make me think that I am under the severe hand of divine justice....

My spirit is always fixed on God, and God is never absent from my mind. However, the more I fix my eyes on him, the more aware I become that he is concealing himself within clouds that are like mists that rise from the dewy earth at sunrise.

The heavenly Father is still having me participate in the sufferings of his only-begotten Son, including physically. That suffering is so intense it cannot be described or imagined. I do not know whether it is through lack of strength or through some fault of my own that, when I am in that state, I cry involuntarily like a baby.

(To Fr. Benedetto of San Marco in Lamis, March 6, 1917)

March 8

Oh God, I do not want to despair, and I do not want to insult your infinite mercy. Nevertheless, despite all my efforts at trusting you, I vividly and clearly sense the bleakness of your abandonment and your rejection....

Oh my God! If you could at the very least let me know that my condition is not a rejection by you and that I am not offending you, I would be willing to suffer this martyrdom a hundred times over....

Help me, father, with your prayers and the prayers of others. I want so much not to feel this very bitter pain! I left everything to please God, and I would have given him my life a thousand times to seal my love for him. But now, oh God, how painful it is when I sense in the depth of my heart that he is angry with me. I am not able, no, not at all, to find peace in my unfortunate state.

(To Fr. Benedetto of San Marco in Lamis, February 20, 1922)

March 9

The glorified Jesus is beautiful, but it seems to me that the crucified Jesus is even more so.

Therefore, my son, love being on the cross more than being at the foot of the cross; love being in agony with Jesus in the garden more than having empathy for him in the garden, because you will resemble the Divine Prototype more this way....

My very dear son, haven't I often taught you to strip yourself of everything that is not of God in order to clothe yourself with our crucified Lord? Come now, God is the one who is allowing this dryness and darkness in your heart. This is not harshness on his part but a kindness. Do not be discouraged on your path, because your situation is pleasing to God. Provided that you are faithful to him at all times, he will not weigh you down more than you can stand, and he will carry the burden with you when he sees that you are shouldering the burden willingly.

(To Br. Emmanuele of San Marco la Catola, January 20, 1918)

March 10

It is good to aspire to absolute Christian perfection, but it is not necessary to overanalyze our improvements and our daily progress, since we entrust the outcome of our aspirations to God's providence. Let us abandon ourselves into his fatherly arms the way little children would. In order to grow, children eat what their father sets before them every day, trusting it will be proportionate to their appetites and needs.

Guard yourself from having scruples and an anxious conscience. Be entirely at peace about what I am telling you, for I am saying it on behalf of Our Lord. Be in God's presence in the ways that I have told you about and in ways that you already knew.

Guard yourself from sadness and worry, because nothing will impede your journey to perfection more.

(To Br. Emmanuele of San Marco la Catola, January 20, 1918)

March 11

What can I tell you about the current state of my soul? The terrible crisis mentioned in my other letter is continually increasing. My soul is presently bound by a circle of iron. I fear offending God in almost everything, and that thought causes me so much terror that I can only compare it to the sufferings of the damned.

My father, do not think I am exaggerating when I say this, because I know what I am talking about. One night it was as though I had died and the Lord made me experience the pains that the damned are suffering there.

However, what torments me even more at this time is an increase in my desire to love God and to respond to his blessings.

(To Fr. Benedetto of San Marco in Lamis, March 11, 1915)

March 12

The apostle Paul tells us, "If we live by the Spirit, let us also walk by the Spirit" [Galatians 5:25].... Do we want to live spiritually, that is, moved and led by the Holy Spirit? We are instructed to mortify the self, which puffs us up, which makes us impetuous, which makes us spiritually dry. In brief, we need to take concern to resist self-conceit, anger, and envy. These three malignant spirits have enslaved the majority of human beings and are extremely opposed to the Spirit of the Lord.

(To Raffaelina Cerase, October 23, 1914)

March 13

Be steadfast in whatever state Jesus is pleased to place you in order to make your heart completely his. Nothing is better than this. Take to him all the things that enslave you, so that you can continually renounce earthly affections. Be assured that the King of heaven will give you regal affections instead to draw you to his holy love.

I see a deep resolution in your heart to want to serve God. That assures me that you will be faithful in the exercise of spiritual devotions and in the constant practice of acquiring virtue. But I do caution you about one thing that you are certainly aware of. When failures occur because of flawed motives on your part, there is no need to be surprised. On the one hand, hate the offense that it gives to God; on the other hand, have a joyful humility, because then you are seeing and understanding your spiritual poverty.

(To Erminia Gargani, January 12, 1917)

March 14

Trust and love, my daughter, have trust and love toward the goodness of our God. You are suffering, but be consoled because you are suffering with Jesus and for Jesus. It is not a punishment but evidence of your salvation.

Be persuaded, because I assure you, on behalf of the Lord, that Jesus is there in the midst of your pain, even at the center of your heart. You are not separated by any distance from the love of such a good God. You experience delight in thinking about God, but you are suffering because you are far from possessing him completely and because you see him being offended by so many ungrateful people. However, things cannot be otherwise than this, my daughter, for whoever loves suffers. This is an immutable law for any pilgrim soul on its journey....

...My lovely daughter, while you are in this state of affliction, keep praying for everyone, especially sinners, to make amends for so many offenses to the divine heart.

(To Maria Gargani, April 9, 1918)

March 15

Let us remember that the destiny of elect souls is to suffer. It is through our suffering in a Christian way that God, the author of all grace and of every gift that leads to salvation, has determined to give us glory. Let us lift up our hearts, then, with complete trust in God alone. Let us humble ourselves under his mighty hand. Let us cheerfully accept the tribulations that the kindness of the heavenly Father sends us, so that he can exalt us during the time of his visitation. Let our only concern be this: to love God and to please him. Let us not be concerned about anything else, knowing that God will always have us in his care more than we can ask or imagine.

(To Raffaelina Cerase, November 26, 1914)

March 16

Oh, how wonderful and gentle is our divine Master's sweet invitation: "If any man would come after me, let him deny himself and take up his cross and follow me" [Matthew 16:24]. This is the invitation that led St. Teresa of Avila to pray to the divine Bridegroom to let her suffer or die…. It was because of this invitation that our seraphic brother St. Francis exclaimed in ecstasy that the good he was awaiting was so great that every pain was a delight to him.

Let us not complain about whatever afflictions or infirmities it might please Jesus to send us. Let us follow the divine Master on the road to Calvary and carry our cross. And if it pleases him to put us on the cross, …let us thank him and consider ourselves fortunate that such honor is shown to us. We know that being on the cross with Jesus is ultimately the most perfect place from which to contemplate him.

(To Raffaelina Cerase, November 26, 1914)

March 17

I exhort you to hold firm to what I told you. The wooden plank that will carry you safely into the harbor of salvation, the divine weapon that will lead to a victory song, is the complete, unquestioning submission of our judgment to the dictates of the one who is charged to guide us through the shadows, perplexities, and battles of life….

If Jesus reveals himself to you, thank him, and if he hides himself from you, thank him for that too—it is all part of his game of love. It is my hope that, when you reach the point of being with Jesus on the cross, you can softly exclaim with Jesus, "It is finished" [John 19:30].

(To Raffaelina Cerase, May 19, 1914)

March 18

"My son," Jesus said," I need sacrificial victims to calm the just and divine anger of my Father. Renew the sacrifice of your whole self to me, and do it without reservation."

I did renew the sacrifice of my life to him, my father, and I feel a sense of sadness in contemplating the God of Sorrows.

If you can, try to find souls who can offer themselves to the Lord as sacrifices for sinners. Jesus will help you.

(To Fr. Agostino of San Marco in Lamis, March 12, 1913)

March 19

The devil, dear father, continues to engage me in war, and unfortunately he is not willing to accept defeat. In the first days of my testing, I confess a weakness in that I was somewhat melancholic. However, the melancholy lifted little by little, and I began to feel myself a bit comforted. Praying at the feet of Jesus, I seemed no longer to feel the weight of fatigue—which I usually feel in conquering myself when I am tempted—or the bitterness of regrets.

The temptations concerning my life in the world are touching my heart more, clouding my mind more, and putting me in a cold sweat; you could say they make me tremble from head to foot. At those times my eyes are good only for weeping. I comfort and encourage myself only by thinking about what you have told me in your letters.

Even in approaching the altar, good God! I feel those attacks, but I have Jesus with me, so what is there to fear?

(To Fr. Benedetto of San Marco in Lamis, March 19, 1911)

March 20

Live at peace, and do not worry about anything. Jesus is with you and loves you, and you are responding to the inspirations and graces that are operating in you. Continue to obey despite internal conflicts and the absence of the consolation that normally comes from obedience and the spiritual life. It is written that those who obey do not need to account for their actions and should await a reward from God and not punishment....

Always keep before your mind's eye the obedience of Jesus in the garden and on the cross; he obeyed in immense conflict with no respite.... Jesus' obedience was excellent, and the more bitter it was, the more beautiful it was. Your soul has never been more acceptable to God than it is now that you are obeying and serving God in dryness and out of sheer faith. Am I being clear here? Be peaceful and joyful, and do not have any doubts at all about the assurances of the one who is now guiding your soul.

(To Maria Gargani, September 4, 1916)

March 21

I know only too well that the cross is the pledge of love, the down payment of forgiveness. Love that is not nourished and fed by the cross is not genuine love; it is nothing but a flash in the pan. And so, knowing this, the false disciple of the Nazarene feels the cross weigh heavily on his heart and—do not be shocked or horrified, my father, at what I am going to say here—many times that false disciple goes in search of a sympathetic Simon of Cyrene to comfort and console him.

What value could my love have for God? I am quite concerned that my love for God be genuine love. This is one of the swords, among many, that pierce me at certain times, and I almost feel on the brink of being overwhelmed.

Nevertheless, father, I have a very great desire to suffer for love of Jesus. So how is it, then, that when I am tested I seek some kind of comfort against my will?…

Write to me when Jesus wants you to, and write as much as you want. I wait for your responses on so many problems, doubts, and difficulties. Your responses are like light from heaven, like refreshing dew to a thirsty plant.

(To Fr. Agostino of San Marco in Lamis, April 21, 1915)

March 22

Writing to the Romans, the holy apostle asks, "Do you not know that all of us who have been baptized into Christ Jesus were baptized into his death?" [Romans 6:3].

Therefore, according to St. Paul, baptism, through which we become children of God and heirs of his kingdom, is a type of, a participation in, a copy of Christ's death. Baptism is a type of the death of Jesus Christ, because, just as Jesus suffered on the cross, so too our baptism is conferred on us with the Sign of the Cross. Just as Jesus was buried in the earth, so too are we immersed in the water of holy baptism.

Baptism is a participation in the death of Jesus because it implements the mysteries of the cross by producing the effects of the death of our Redeemer. The death of Christ is applied to us in baptism in such a way that it is as if his death were our death and we were crucified with him. In virtue of his death, all our sins are cancelled in terms of guilt and punishment.

(To Raffaelina Cerase, September 19, 1914)

March 23

We have two lives. The natural one from Adam through the flesh is an earthly, corruptible life that we are fond of and that is full of base passions. The other life is the supernatural one from Jesus through baptism, so it is a spiritual, heavenly life that operates by virtue. A real transformation occurs in us through baptism: We die to sin and become one with Jesus Christ in such a way that we share in his very own life. In baptism we receive the sanctifying grace that gives us a heavenly life. It makes us sons and daughters of God, brothers and sisters of Jesus, and heirs of heaven.

Now, if every Christian is able to die to the first life and be resurrected into the second life through baptism, then the duty of every Christian is to seek after the things that belong to heaven and to have no concern for the things of this earth. This is exactly what Paul says to the Colossians: "If then you have been raised with Christ," this great saint says, "seek the things that are above" [Colossians 3:1].

(To Raffaelina Cerase, November 16, 1914)

March 24

Christians must guard themselves from vice if they want to live according to the Spirit of Jesus Christ. Vices and sins constitute the old man, the earthly man, the flesh. The apostle wants all Christians to strip themselves of it: "Put off the old man with his practices" [Colossians 3:9]. Christians, then, having died and been raised with Jesus through baptism, should strive to renew themselves and seek perfection by contemplating eternal truths and God's desires. They should, in a word, always strive to have the likeness of the Creator restored in themselves.

Insofar as the apostle commands us to seek Christian perfection, he motivates us with this very wise saying: "Put on the new man, who is being renewed in knowledge after the image of his creator" [Colossians 3:10]. But who is this new man that Paul is talking about here? It is the person sanctified by baptism and who, according to the principles of sanctification, should live in "true righteousness and holiness" [Ephesians 4:24].

(To Raffaelina Cerase, November 16, 1914)

March 25

As soon as I begin to pray, my heart is invaded by a fire of living love. This flame has nothing whatsoever to do with flames of this world below. It is a delicate, sweet flame that consumes but causes no pain at all. It is so sweet and delightful that, although the soul experiences great pleasure in it and is content, it still does not lose the intense desire for it. Oh God! This is so marvelous that I may never understand it until I am in my heavenly home.

That desire for more, far from impinging on the complete content-ment the soul experiences, refines the soul even more. The enjoyment the soul feels, rather than being diminished by the desire, becomes even more intense.

(To Fr. Benedetto of San Marco in Lamis, March 26, 1914)

March 26

The soul that the Lord places in such a state and enriches with such heavenly experiences should be more loquacious. But no, my soul has become almost mute. I do not know if this phenomenon is happening only to me. I succeed in expressing—in rather generic terms and most often without making much sense—only a very small part of what my soul's Bridegroom is doing.

Believe me, my father, my inability to do so is not a light torment for my soul. What happens to me could be compared to the experience of a poor shepherd boy who is brought into a royal exhibition room full of precious objects that are "out of this world" and that he has never seen before. After leaving that room, the boy would certainly have in his mind all those precious and beautiful objects, but he certainly would not know the exact number of them or what names to call them. He would want to tell others about everything he saw and would marshal his intellectual and analytical strength to describe them. Then, seeing that all his attempts would not succeed in making himself understood, he prefers to keep silent.

(To Fr. Benedetto of San Marco in Lamis, March 26, 1914)

March 27

It seems that God has poured out into the depths of my heart many graces of compassion for the misery of others, especially for the needy and the poor. The intense compassion that I feel when I see a poor person ignites a vehement desire in my heart to help him. If it were up to me alone, I would rush to take off my clothes in order to clothe that needy man.

If I know that some man is afflicted, whether in body or in soul, what would I not do in the Lord to see him set free of his troubles? I would willingly take on all his afflictions in order to see him spared, offering the fruit of my suffering on his behalf, if the Lord allowed me to do that....

I see full well that this is a very special favor from God, because, before this, although through his divine mercy I never overlooked helping the needy, I had very little or no pity for their troubles.

(To Fr. Benedetto of San Marco in Lamis, March 26, 1914)

March 28

Friday morning I was still in bed when Jesus appeared to me. He was sad and downcast. He showed me a large number of order and regular priests, several of whom were ecclesiastical dignitaries. Some of them were celebrating Mass, some were putting on their vestments for Mass, and some were removing them. Seeing Jesus in anguish caused me much pain, so I asked him why he was suffering so much. I received no answer. His gaze was still turned toward these priests. Shortly after, as if he were weary of looking and somewhat appalled, he withdrew his gaze from them and fixed it on me. I was horrified to see two tears streaming down his face. He moved away from that crowd of priests with an expression of disgust on his face and exclaimed, "Butchers!" Turning to me he said, "My son, do not think that my agony lasted for three hours. No. I will be in agony until the end of the world on behalf of the souls that have been most blessed by me.... The ingratitude and the drowsiness of my ministers make my agony more burdensome.

"Oh! How badly they respond to my love! What pains me most is that they add disrespect and unbelief to their indifference...."

Jesus is right to complain about our ingratitude!

(To Fr. Agostino of San Marco in Lamis, April 7, 1913)

March 29

You ask me to evaluate your love for God. My dearest son, why don't you feel that very love in your spirit? What is this burning desire that you are talking to me about? Who has put that yearning to love Our Lord in your heart? Don't holy desires come from him? Even if someone has only a yearning to love God, that is enough. It comes from God himself, because God is present wherever there is a desire for his love. Therefore be at peace about the presence of divine charity in your heart. And if your longing is not satisfied, if it seems to you that you are always desiring but never reaching and possessing perfect love, that does not prove the absence of your love for God. Rather it just means that you should never say, "I have enough." It just means that you should not and cannot stop on your journey toward divine love and holy perfection.

Yearn for him always, yearn with greater confidence, and do not be afraid.

(To Br. Emmanuele of San Marco la Catola, March 29, 1918)

March 30

My son, you can be certain of this: God can reject everything about a human being conceived in sin and carrying the indelible mark inherited from Adam, but he absolutely cannot reject a sincere desire to love him. Therefore, if you cannot be reassured about your heavenly favor with God for other reasons, and if your trust in the one speaking to you in the name of God does not relieve or comfort you, then at least be reassured about it because of your sincere desire to love him.

I urge you in the name of God not to let yourself be overcome by the fear that I see in your letters—the fear of not loving and not fearing God—because it seems to me that the enemy wants to lead you into some kind of deception. I know, my son, that no one can worthily love God. However, when a soul does all it can and does it with a sincere intention and trust in divine mercy, why would God reject that person? Hasn't God told us to love him with all our strength? If you have given everything and consecrated everything to God, what is there to fear? Are you perhaps afraid you cannot do more than you are doing now? But Jesus is not asking more of you now, so he will not be able to condemn you.

(To Br. Emmanuele of San Marco la Catola, March 29, 1918)

March 31

Dearest father,

As I remember the many instances of care you have shown me, I feel a sacred duty, now that holy Easter is approaching, not to let it go by without wishing you the fullness of all those graces that can make us joyful here on earth and blessed in heaven.

That is my hope for you, my father, and I believe it will be welcomed by you. At this solemn time I will not fail, despite my unworthiness, to pray to the risen Jesus for your beautiful soul, although I never forget to pray for you every day.

During these holy days more than ever, I am extremely afflicted by that wicked devil. Therefore I ask you to entrust me fervently to the Lord so that I do not continue to be a victim of our common enemy.

God, however, is with me, and the consolations I enjoy from him are so sweet that I cannot describe them.

(To Fr. Benedetto of San Marco in Lamis, March 31, 1912)

April 1

The Lord is with you; he fights with you and for you. With such a warrior on your side, you can have no doubt about complete victory over that foul and impure apostate, the devil. Groan before Jesus, knock fervently and insistently at his sacred heart, but the response he is sending you through me is no different from what he said to the Apostle to the Gentiles: "My grace is sufficient for you" [2 Corinthians 12:9]. Yes, keep a guard over yourself, flee idleness and all base conversation.... Always remember the apostle's saying that our treasure is kept in a fragile earthen vessel [see 2 Corinthians 4:7]....

Be at peace in all things, because the enemy, who always fishes in troubled waters, takes advantage of our discouragement to achieve his intentions more readily.

(To Fr. Paolino of Casacalenda, March 21, 1916)

April 2

I would like the object of your daily meditations to be the abasement of the Son of God and the glory that was given to him because of it. Let us reflect on the self-emptying of the Word. According to St. Paul, "though he was in the form of God" [Philippians 2:6], and though in him "the whole fulness of deity dwells bodily" [Colossians 2:9], he did not despise the humbling of himself to become like us so that he could bring us the knowledge of God.

The Word, completely and freely, lowered himself to our level, concealing his divine nature under the veil of human flesh. St. Paul says the Word of God "emptied himself, taking the form of a servant" [Philippians 2:7].... He took on the likeness of a human being and subjected himself to hunger, thirst, and fatigue. In the words of the Apostle to the Gentiles, he was "one who in every respect has been tempted as we are, yet without sinning" [Hebrews 4:15].

The culmination of his abasement, however, occurred in his passion and death, in which he subjected himself by his human will to the will of his Father. He underwent so many torments, including suffering the most degrading death of crucifixion: "He humbled himself and became obedient unto death, even death on a cross" [Philippians 2:8].... His obedience was so pleasing to the eternal Father, the apostle says, that he "exalted him and bestowed on him the name which is above every name" [Philippians 2:9].

(To Raffaelina Cerase, November 4, 1914)

April 3

There is only one name in which we can hope for salvation, and the apostles declared that truth to the Jews: "There is no other name under heaven given among men by which we must be saved" [Acts of the Apostles 4:12].

The eternal Father wanted to subject all things to him, so "that at the name of Jesus every knee should bow, in heaven and on earth and under the earth" [Philippians 2:10]. This is what the apostle says, and it is true. Jesus is indeed worshiped in heaven. Moved by gratitude and love, the blessed unendingly sing to him what St. John heard and saw in one of his visions: "They sang a new song, saying, 'Worthy are you to take the scroll and to open its seals, / for you were slain and by your blood you ransomed men for God'" [Revelation 5:9].

This most holy name is reverenced on the earth because all the graces we ask for in the name of Jesus are fully granted by the eternal Father: "If you ask anything of the Father," the divine Master tells us, "he will give it to you in my name" [John 16:23]. This divine name is also venerated—who would imagine it?—even in hell, because that name is the terror of demons, who find themselves overthrown and cast down: "In my name they will cast out demons" [Mark 16:17].

(To Raffaelina Cerase, November 4, 1914)

April 4

Because of Jesus' obedience, the heavenly Father wanted this most holy name to be confessed and believed in by all creatures: "Every tongue [will] confess that Jesus Christ is Lord, to the glory of God the Father" [Philippians 2:11]. And isn't this what we see now that the cross is adored in all places? On the last day even the damned and the demons, seeing the immense glory of Jesus and his infinite power, will have to acquiesce to this veneration as well.

If we are imitators of Jesus Christ as we undergo all the battles of life, we too will participate in his victories.... Let us believe firmly in the holy Redeemer, since there is so much glory adorning him. Let us continue to live for his glory, imitating his example and acting according to his wishes. Otherwise our faith will be of no use if our works do not correspond to our belief.

(To Raffaelina Cerase, November 4, 1914)

April 5

I was hearing the confessions of young people, beginning at 5:00 PM, when all of a sudden I was filled with extreme terror at the sight of a heavenly being who appeared before my mind's eye. He held a kind of instrument in his hand, similar to a long iron spear with a well-honed point, and fire seemed to be coming out of that point.

At the very exact instant I saw this being, I also observed him hurl that instrument with all his might into me. Scarcely had I uttered a groan when I felt as if I was dying. I told the young man in the confessional to leave because I did not feel well and I did not have the strength to continue.

This martyrdom lasted without interruption for a week, until the morning of the seventh day. The things that I suffered during this period are so distressing that I do not know how to tell you about them. I even saw my inner organs ripped out and twisted by this instrument, and all of them were pierced and burned by the lance and its fiery tip. From that day until now I have been mortally wounded. I feel an open wound in the deepest part of my being that makes me constantly writhe in pain.

(To Fr. Benedetto of San Marco in Lamis, August 21, 1918)

April 6

You know that perfect love is acquired when we possess the object of our love. So why do you have so much fruitless anxiety and discouragement? Always long for more love with complete confidence, and do not be afraid.

…I know that no pilgrim soul can worthily love God. But when a soul does all it can and trusts in divine mercy, why would Jesus reject it? Didn't God command us to love him with all our strength? If you have given all and consecrated all to God, why be afraid?… Tell Jesus, "Do you want more love from me? I don't have any more to give. Give me more love, and I will offer it back to you!" Have no doubt that Jesus will accept that offer.

(To Erminia Gargani, December 14, 1916)

April 7

The spring is already past and is long gone. My soul was deaf to the voice of the Bridegroom when he lovingly invited me to follow him after the harsh season was over, after winter had passed. My soul adorned itself all through the spring, but it slept the sleep of the ungrateful, and it awoke too late. My soul sought my beloved everywhere, and thanks to God's mercy, my soul found him seated in the midst of many lovers whose hands were full of flowers offering him their fragrance.

My soul acknowledged its mistake and determined to follow after him. I took the last place in line. Even now, though, my soul does not know what to offer him, since it has nothing of its own to offer. And yet be amazed at the goodness of this divine lover, who does not push away my soul but draws it to himself with loving qualities. My God, how does one respond to such perfect love?

(To Raffaelina Cerase, December 12, 1914)

April 8

Do not lose heart because of your minor imperfections. Try to be vigilant over yourself so that you do not fall short. But when you see yourself fail, do not get entangled in useless arguments. Instead kneel before God, be ashamed of your lack of constancy, and humble yourself profoundly. Ask Our Lord for forgiveness, and plan to be more vigilant in the future. Then get up immediately and move forward on the path I laid out for you.

Understand, my very delightful daughter, that failures and minor surges of passion are inevitable as long as we are still on this earth. This is the reason the great apostle St. Paul exclaims to heaven, "Wretched man that I am!" [Romans 7:24]. There are two lives in me, he says, the old and the new; two laws, the law of the flesh and the law of the spirit; two things working in me, nature and grace. "Who will deliver me from this body of death?" [Romans 7:24].

(To Rachelina Russo, September 25, 1917)

April 9

My daughter, you need to accept what we have inherited from our ancestors, Adam and Eve. Self-love never dies before we do and will accompany us to the grave. My God, my daughter, what unhappiness belongs to us poor children of Eve! We will feel the palpable attacks of self-love and its secret workings throughout our unfortunate exile. So what do we do now? Should we become discouraged and lose heart and renounce the path to heaven? No, my most beloved daughter, let us take courage. It is sufficient that we do not consent to self-love in a deliberate, forceful, and ongoing way.

(To Rachelina Russo, September 25, 1917)

April 10

Be vigilant. Do not ever give in completely to yourself, and do not put your trust in yourself. Seek at all times to try to advance on the path of perfection and to abound more and more in charity, which is the bond of Christian perfection. Abandon yourself into the arms of the heavenly Father with childlike trust, and open your heart to the charisms of the Holy Spirit, who is waiting for your consent to enrich you with them.

(To Raffaelina Cerase, December 10, 1914)

April 11

We Christians are doubly made in the image of God. First, we are in his image through nature insofar as we have been given intelligence, memory, and will. Second, we are in his image through grace, because sanctification through baptism leaves the most beautiful image of God imprinted on our souls. Yes, my dear, sanctifying grace has imprinted on us the image of God to such an extent that we ourselves almost become gods through participation. I am referring to St. Peter's lovely expression that we have now become "partakers of the divine nature" [2 Peter 1:4].

You see, my sister, how great our dignity is. We are great, however, only if we keep that sanctifying grace.

(To Raffaelina Cerase, November 16, 1914)

April 12

Continue to obey, and you will be assured of the best reward that is promised to a soul who loves Jesus. You should not allow any turmoil to enter your soul for any reason…. I understand that the soul in which God dwells can at every step be fearful of offending God, but this holy fear can become almost deadly if it blocks the fulfilling of our duties. However, be comforted that it is precisely because of this fear that you will not fall into error if you keep pushing forward. My brother, if being able to stand depended on us, we would fall into the hands of the enemies of our salvation at the least little thing. Let us always put our trust in the goodness of God, and we will experience more and more how good the Lord is.

(To Fr. Basilio of Mirabello Sannitico, February 9, 1916)

April 13

Flee turmoil and anxiety with all your strength. Otherwise all your spiritual efforts will have little success or bear no fruit. We know for certain that when our spirit is in distress, the attacks of the enemy are more frequent and more direct. He profits from our natural weakness to succeed in his purposes. Let us be on the alert about this very important point. Whenever we fall into discouragement, let us stir up our faith and entrust ourselves to the arms of the heavenly Father, who is always ready to receive whoever sincerely comes to him.

(To Fr. Basilio of Mirabello Sannitico, February 9, 1916)

April 14

You are restless to be free of the enemies that surround you because those apostles of Satan are all intent on making you transgress. As for the grief you still feel about being surrounded by opportunities to offend God, I tell you those occasions are the result of divine graces that the very good Lord has abundantly sown in your heart.

This is all a very certain sign that the love the Holy Spirit has poured into your soul is not lifeless but very alert. Your longings, in the context of a humility that comes from a modest opinion of yourself, cannot in any way come from demonic deception. Your desire to be free of enemies who want you to transgress and offend God and your desire to avoid the occasions that test your faithfulness absolutely rule out that this is a strategy of the enemy. He does not have and, therefore, cannot engender such sentiments.

(To Raffaelina Cerase, July 28, 1914)

April 15

Hasn't Our Lord promised that he is faithful and will not permit us ever to be overcome? "God is faithful, and he will not let you be tempted beyond your strength, but with the temptation will also provide the way of escape, that you may be able to endure it" [1 Corinthians 10:13].

How can you believe otherwise, my sister? Isn't God far kinder than we can imagine? Isn't he more interested in our salvation than we are? How many times has he proved that to us? How many victories has he won for you over some rather powerful enemies and even over yourself through the help of his grace, without which you would inevitably have been crushed?

Let us ponder Jesus' love for us and his zeal for our well-being, and let us be calm because of that, not doubting that he will help us with more than fatherly protection against all our enemies.

(To Raffaelina Cerase, July 28, 1914)

April 16

When Mass was over [last Tuesday], I was talking to Jesus and giving him thanks. Oh, how sweet the conversation with paradise was that morning! Although I would like to try to explain it all, I cannot. There are things that cannot be put into human language without losing their profound heavenly meaning. Jesus' heart and mine were fused together—if you allow me to express it that way. No longer were there two hearts beating but only one. My heart had disappeared, like a drop of water that is engulfed in the sea. The sea of paradise was Jesus, the King. The joy in me was so intense and profound that I could not contain it. Tears of delight streamed down my face.

Yes, papa, people cannot understand that, when paradise is poured into a heart that is sorrowful, exiled, weak, and mortal, it cannot be contained without tears. Yes, I repeat, the very joy that filled my heart made me weep at length.

(To Fr. Agostino of San Marco in Lamis, April 18, 1912)

April 17

Let your whole life be spent in self-surrender, in prayer, in work, in humility, in giving thanks to our good God. If you ever feel impatience rising up again, go to prayer immediately. Remember, we are always in God's presence, and he is the one to whom we must render an account for all our actions, good or bad. Above all, meditate on the abasement that the Son of God suffered out of love for us. I would like Jesus' sufferings and humiliations to be the daily theme for your meditations. If you do that, as I am sure you will, you will experience good fruit in a very short time. That sort of meditation will be a shield with which to defend yourself from impatience whenever our sweetest Jesus sends you difficulties or causes you to experience desolation.

(To Annita Rodote, February 6, 1915)

April 18

You need to keep yourself far away from three things. First, keep yourself from ever quarreling or being in strife with anybody. If you conduct yourself otherwise, you can say farewell to peace and charity....

Second, keep yourself from vainglory, or self-conceit, which is the vice that attacks devout people the most. Without our noticing it, this vice nudges us to want to stand out more than others and to want others to admire us. Even St. Paul warns his beloved Philippians about this: "Do nothing from selfishness or conceit" [Philippians 2:3].... Self-abnegation that considers others better than yourself is the only remedy for this vice.

You need to guard against a third thing that is no less dangerous than self-conceit because it contains the hellish seed of division: Never put your welfare ahead of that of others, because it always and necessarily tends to break the beautiful bond of love, the bond that should always unite Christians. In St. Paul's words, love "binds everything together in perfect harmony" [Colossians 3:14].

(To Raffaelina Cerase, November 4, 1914)

April 19

Even as I write to you, my father, where do my thoughts fly? To the wonderful day of my ordination [August 10, 1910]. Tomorrow, the feast of St. Lawrence, is the anniversary of that day, and I am already experiencing anew the joy of that day that is so sacred for me. Since this morning I have begun to taste paradise.... What will it be like for us to enjoy it eternally? As I compare the peace that I felt in my heart on that day with the peace that I began to feel in my heart since yesterday, there is no difference.

The feast of St. Lawrence was the day my heart was most enkindled with love for Jesus. How happy I was, and how I delighted in that day!

(To Fr. Agostino of San Marco in Lamis, August 9, 1912)

April 20

God wanted to win us to himself by having us experience abundant blessings and consolations in our wills and in our hearts during all our devotions. But who cannot see how much danger surrounds that kind of love of God? It would be easy for a poor soul to attach itself to the sweet consolations in devotions and in loving God without attending in the least to genuine devotion and the essential love of God, which is the only thing that makes a soul beloved and accepted by God.

Our very tender Lord comes quickly with loving concern to deal with this very great peril. When he sees that a soul is well established in his love, is affectionately joined to him, keeps itself far from earthly things and the occasions of sin, has acquired enough virtue to maintain itself in his holy service without the sweet attractions of the senses, he wants to advance that soul to a higher degree of holiness. He then removes those sweet signs of affection that the soul has experienced in meditation, prayer, and other devotions until that point. What is the most painful for a person in this state is the loss of a capacity for prayer and meditation and being left in darkness and a completely distressing state of dryness....What that person calls abandonment, however, is nothing other than the heavenly Father's very special and solicitous care.

(To Raffaelina Cerase, January 9, 1915)

April 21

How is it, my father, that when I am with Jesus, not everything I resolutely intended to ask him comes to mind? This lapse of memory causes me very great distress. What can explain that? No one has been able to explain it fully to me up to this point.

I also experience something else that is rather odd. When I am with Jesus, I end up asking him things that I had never thought of before and interceding not only for people whom I did not have in mind—and this causes me to wonder the most—but also people whom I have never even met or heard of before.

I have also observed that when these things happen, as far as I can tell, Jesus always grants me what I ask for on behalf of these people.

(To Fr. Benedetto of San Marco in Lamis, April 21, 1915)

April 22

What joy it is to serve Jesus in the desert without manna, water, and other consolations, other than being under his guidance and suffering for him!…

During this state of dryness and desolation of spirit, do not become agitated that you are not serving God the way you want to, because as you adapt yourself to his will, you are actually serving him the way he wants you to, which is so much better. We should not be worried or anxious if we are serving God in one way rather than another. Actually, because he is the only thing we are seeking, and since we do not find him any less when we walk through the parched desert than when we walk on the water of sweet consolation, we should be as content with one path as with another.

(To Lucia Fiorentino, January 11, 1917)

April 23

Continue to cry out with the apostle that you are "always carrying in the body the death of Jesus" [2 Corinthians 4:10], because that is the most consistent groan of your spirit now. You could say, "I have become one with Christ in spirit on the cross," until the time comes when you will say, "Father, into your hands I commit my spirit!" [Luke 23:46].

I know, though, that you want to hasten the moment of being able to say the above verse. However, my daughter, can you really say, "*Consummatum est*" ["It is finished" (John 19:30)]? It might seem that way to you, but not to me. Your mission is not yet complete, and you must thirst for the salvation of your brothers and sisters more than you want to be taken up into God.

(To Margherita Tresca, April 26, 1919)

April 24

Do not worry, my most beloved daughter, about the dryness, the exhaustion, and the troubling shadows that are present in your spirit, because God has willed them for your greater good. One day Mary Magdalene was speaking to the Master, but thinking that she was separated from him, she was weeping and looking for him. She was so eager to see him that, although she was indeed seeing him, she did not see him because she thought he was a gardener.

The same is true for you too. Come now, be courageous, my daughter, and do not worry for nothing. You have the Master as your companion and are not separated from him. That is the truth, the real truth. What are you afraid of? What are you moaning about? You must not be a child or even a woman in this matter; what is needed here is a manly heart. As long as your soul is determined to live and die in serving and loving God, do not be dismayed about either your powerlessness or any other hindrance.

(To Antonietta Vona, August 18, 1918)

April 25

The fear that you have offended God is the surest proof that you have not offended him.

Entrust yourself with boundless confidence to God's goodness. The more the enemy increases his violent attacks against you, the more you should lean confidently on the breast of your very tender heavenly Bridegroom, who will never allow you to be defeated. God himself has solemnly proclaimed this in sacred Scripture: "No temptation has overtaken you that is not common to man. God is faithful, and he will not let you be tempted beyond your strength, but with the temptation will also provide the way of escape, that you may be able to endure it" [1 Corinthians 10:13].

To believe otherwise is disloyalty to God, who has kept us from falling in similar situations. Even St. Paul was restless and asked to be relieved of the difficult test in his flesh,...but was he not assured that the help of grace would always be sufficient for him?

Our enemy, who is committed to our harm, wants to convince you otherwise, but spurn him in the name of Jesus and laugh at him. This is the best remedy for beating him into retreat. He becomes emboldened by our weakness, but when someone confronts him with a weapon in hand, he becomes a coward.

(To Raffaelina Cerase, April 25, 1914)

April 26

Love makes us take giant strides forward, but fear, instead, makes us look cautiously at every little step we take lest we stumble on the path that leads to heaven. I know that the cross is painful, my most beloved sister, and for lovers, whatever could risk offending the one we love and adore becomes almost unbearable. However, Jesus, in his desert temptations and hanging on the cross, is a vivid, clear, and very comforting proof of what I declare to you now in the name of the very tender Bridegroom of souls: The storms of life are indeed present for a soul that seeks God in everything—especially a soul that longs for him, that desires only him in her heart, that longs to have him reign as King at the center of her being, and that ardently desires to be completely and wholly possessed by him…. I tell you, however, this is all a very obvious sign of a special love and exceptional mercy from God's loving providence.

(To Raffaelina Cerase, April 25, 1914)

April 27

Have courage, then, and move forward. God is with you, and the world, the flesh, and the devil, to their dismay, will one day lay down their weapons and confess once more that they can do nothing against a soul who possesses and is possessed by God….

There is open warfare against you, my dear, so you need to be vigilant at all times and to put up strong resistance against it, always having the eyes of faith turned to the Lord of Hosts, who fights with you and for you. Have absolute confidence in the goodness of God that victory is assured. Why should you believe otherwise? Isn't our God more interested in our salvation than we are? Who can resist and ever prevail over the monarch of the heavens? What power do the world, the flesh, and the devil have before the Lord?

(To Raffaelina Cerase, April 25, 1914)

April 28

You say that you cannot tell if the rays of light that are coming into the depths of your spirit at times are coming from God or not....

Well, here are three signs by which to discern if these rays of light are from the Father of lights. The first is that such light gives us even more wonderful knowledge of God. To the degree that this knowledge is disclosed to us, it gives us a much deeper understanding of his incomprehensible greatness. That light leads us to love God the Father even more and to sacrifice ourselves even more for his honor and glory. The second sign is an increased knowledge of ourselves, a deeper sense of humility when we realize that such wretched creatures as ourselves have had the impudence to offend him.... The third is that these heavenly rays always produce increasing disdain for the things of this world, except for those things that can be useful for God's service.

If the rays of light produce these three effects, consider them as coming from God. These results cannot be produced by the enemy and even less so by your fantasy and imagination.

(To Raffaelina Cerase, April 25, 1914)

April 29

I urge you to comfort yourself with the splendid thought that your physical and spiritual sufferings are the evidence of God's will for you, in that he wants to make you more conformed to the heavenly prototype, Jesus Christ, through these sufferings....

For those who hope in the Lord, having a tranquil conscience can come only from God himself. I am saying this in answer to your question about this matter.

Feeling no attraction whatsoever to any place in this world below can have no source other than God himself, who wants to detach the soul from everything that is not himself.

(To Raffaelina Cerase, September, 28, 1915)

April 30

The path that the apostle marks out for Christians is to strip themselves of the vices belonging to the old nature, the flesh, and to clothe themselves with the virtues taught by Jesus Christ. In terms of vices Paul says, "Put to death therefore what is earthly in you" [Colossians 3:5]. Although Christians are sanctified through baptism, they are not exempt from the rebellion of the senses and the passions. For this reason there is a pressing need to put them [the senses and passions] to death.

(To Raffaelina Cerase, November 16, 1914)

MAY

May 1

Every soul destined for eternal glory can most surely consider itself a stone destined to be used to help construct the eternal edifice. A brick-layer who wants to build a house must first shape the stones that will be used, and he does this with a hammer and chisel. The heavenly Father does the same thing with elect souls who from all eternity have been destined in his lofty wisdom and providence to be part of the eternal edifice.

Therefore the soul destined to reign with Jesus Christ in eternity must be prepared with a hammer and chisel. How does the divine artist prepare these stones, his elect souls? My sister, his chisel blows are the shadows, the fears, the temptations, the afflictions of the spirit, the deso-lation of spiritual trepidations, and even physical sufferings.

Offer thanksgiving to the infinite mercy of the eternal Father who is treating you this way.

(To Raffaelina Cerase, May 19, 1914)

May 2

Because of the way that grace is operating in you, you have every reason to be comforted and to hope and trust in God. This is generally the way grace works in souls who have chosen him as their portion and inheritance. The prototype, the example we need to mirror and to model in our lives, is Jesus Christ. Jesus chose the cross as his standard, and he wants all his followers to walk the road to Calvary, carrying the cross so that they can then be stretched out on it. This road alone leads to salvation.

(To Maria Gargani, September 4, 1916)

May 3

Remember the goodness of the Lord in his treatment of you up until now. He will continue his work of perfection to your benefit. He will continue to pour out abundantly on you not only the oil of his mercy to make you rejoice but also the oil of his power to make you strong to fight successfully. It is said that wrestlers rubbed oil on their limbs to make themselves more agile, more flexible, and sturdier.

Live at peace, because divine compassion is never lacking and certainly will not be lacking to you if you show yourself docile to his divine workings. Come now, Raffaelina, do not be stingy with the heavenly physician. For love's sake, do not make him wait for you any longer. "Give me your heart" [Proverbs 23:26], he is saying to you. "Give me your heart, my daughter, so that I may pour out my oil on it."

(To Raffaelina Cerase, August 4, 1915)

May 4

Always keep your life united to Jesus Christ in the olive garden where he agonized and suffered. Participating there in the anointing of his grace and the comfort of his strength, you will later find yourself in that same olive garden after death, but participating in the joys of his ascension and glory....

Understand, then, how to suffer in a wholly Christian manner, and do not be afraid, because no suffering, no matter how vile its source, will go unrewarded in eternal life. Trust and hope in the merits of Jesus, and even our humble clay will become refined gold that shines in the royal palace of the monarch of the heavens.

(To Raffaelina Cerase, August 4, 1915)

May 5

My dear, we can never have too much of that virtue [of charity], although I see you are well advanced in it. Nevertheless, I will never cease to add my exhortation to you to abound in love more and more, since that is the divine Master's favorite virtue and the one he most often counsels us to have. He wanted this virtue to be the guiding principle for all his followers. This precept of charity [to love one another as he loved us] finds its source in him and is an innovation, since it was unknown to the majority of the patriarchs of the old covenant.

(To Raffaelina Cerase, December 12, 1914)

May 6

How bitter the thought is, daughter, of having to give account to God for sins that we made others commit because of the wrong direction in which we were going....

You cannot know what a thorn this concern is for me. It is always embedded at the core of my spirit, and it makes me suffer at every moment. A thousand of the most excruciating deaths would count for very little in the face of this new cross sent to me by God—a cross, if I am not mistaken, that will accompany me to my death.

I know this thorn will eat away at me slowly, because it is not a temptation but instead something directly willed by God....

All my strength is useless in removing or even diminishing this very painful thorn. It does not leave me for an instant.

(To Girolama Longo, April 15, 1918)

May 7

How good the Lord is to everyone! But how much more does he demonstrate that goodness to those who have a genuine and sincere desire to please him in everything and await the fulfillment of his divine purposes in them!

Learn to recognize and worship God's will even more concerning all human events. Often repeat the divine words of our dearest Master: "Thy will be done, / On earth as it is in heaven" [Matthew 6:10]. May this lovely prayer always be in your heart and on your lips in all the circumstances of your life. Repeat these words when you are afflicted; repeat them when you are tempted and when you undergo trials that Jesus sends you. Repeat them even when you are engulfed in the ocean of Jesus' love. That prayer will be your anchor and your salvation.

(To Annita Rodote, February 6, 1915)

May 8

My heart is overflowing with joy and feels increasingly stronger to face any affliction as long as it pleases Jesus.

This is also the case because the devil is giving himself no rest to make me lose my peace and to diminish the great trust I have in divine mercy. The devil is primarily trying to remove my peace and trust through constant temptations against holy purity by stirring up my imagination; at other times he does so whenever I merely glance at things that I would not call holy but are at least neutral.

I laugh about all this as something not to be too concerned about, just as you have counseled me. The only thing that concerns me at times is that I am not sure I resisted the initial assault of the enemy immediately. As I examine myself, I am sure that I would prefer to die rather than to offend my dear Jesus deliberately by a single sin, even a minor one.

(To Fr. Benedetto of San Marco in Lamis, August 17, 1914)

May 9

Jesus makes you more precious to himself and more like himself through the paths of sorrow....

Unfortunately, we need a lot of strength to walk those paths. However, take heart, because the Savior's assistance to you will not diminish. Therefore, let us hasten to unite ourselves, to be part of that group of pious and faithful souls who draw near to the divine Master. Let us hasten, I repeat, so that we do not lag too far behind this holy company. Let us always keep ourselves united to such people and not lose sight of them. Let us never lift our gaze from them, lest we are unable to reach them, lest we remain deprived of those secret treasures of blessings that are found only in their midst, lest we remain excluded from the eternal joy that we can succeed in possessing only through them and with them.

(To Raffaelina Cerase, August 4, 1915)

May 10

Holiness means overcoming ourselves. It means having perfect victory over all our passions. It means truly and constantly disregarding ourselves and despising the things of this world to the point of preferring poverty to riches, humiliation to glory, and pain to pleasure. Holiness means loving our neighbor as ourselves out of love for God. With regard to others, holiness means loving even those who curse us, who hate us, who persecute us, and even doing good to them. Holiness means living a life of humility, detachment, wisdom, righteousness, patience, charity, chastity, gentleness, and diligence. It is a life of doing our duty for no other reason than to please God and receive our reward from him alone.

In summary, Raffaelina, holiness has the power in itself, according to the language of the sacred books, to transform a human being into God.

(To Raffaelina Cerase, December 30, 1915)

May 11

There are three great truths that we must especially pray for the Holy Paraclete to reveal to us. First, let us pray that he makes us understand more and more the excellence of our Christian calling. To have been chosen, to have been elected from among so many, and to know that this election, not through any merit of our own, was made by God from eternity "before the foundation of the world" [Ephesians 1:4] so that we would belong to him in time and eternity! This is such a great mystery, and it is also so sweet that, as soon as we barely penetrate that mystery, we cannot help but completely melt with love.

Second, let us pray that he reveal to us more and more the greatness of the eternal inheritance that our heavenly Father has destined for us. Penetrating this mystery draws us away from earthly goods and makes us eager to arrive at our heavenly home.

Finally, let us pray to the Father of lights that he make us penetrate more and more the mystery of our justification by which we, wretched sinners, are brought to salvation. Our justification is such a great mystery that sacred Scripture compares it to the resurrection of the divine Master.

(To Raffaelina Cerase, October 23, 1914)

May 12

Our justification from unrighteousness is so monumental that we can easily say God demonstrated more of his power in justifying us than in creating the heavens and the earth out of nothing. There is a bigger contrast between a sinner and grace than there is between nothingness and being. There is more distance between a sinner and God than there is between nothingness and God. In fact, nothingness, being the deprivation of being, has no power to resist God's will, whereas a sinner, a being with a free will, can resist all of God's wishes. In addition, creation belongs to the natural order of things, whereas the justification of the ungodly belongs to the supernatural and divine order.

Oh! If only everyone could understand the depth of the wretchedness and degradation from which God's omnipotent hand has rescued us. Oh! If we could fully comprehend only for an instant the new status to which God's grace has raised us, which still amazes angels! He has raised us to the status of being nothing less than his sons and daughters now destined to reign with his Son for all eternity!

(To Raffaelina Cerase, October 23, 1914)

May 13

The first and primary principle to keep in mind is obedience, obedience at all times in submitting your whole self. Therefore, in your activities you must not overanalyze things, so set aside whatever doubt assails you without becoming anxious, and chase it away with holy obedience. Jesus will always be pleased with whatever you do. Avoid only what you clearly know to be sin.... Take note that I said Jesus will always be pleased with whatever you do, because when your habitual will is to please God, and when you are assured of having that disposition—and I assure you again now that you do have it—then every action of yours will be pleasing to him. It should not matter to you if you are not able to see this yourself; Jesus is standing guard over your will, which is disposed to please him at all times.

(To Luigi Bozzutto, November 25, 1917)

May 14

Consider as suspect all those desires that wise and pious souls say cannot produce the intended effects. In that category you will find desires for a certain kind of Christian perfection that can be imagined but never practiced.... Therefore, set aside the concern you told me about regarding what you have read in books. Reflect soberly on the vanity of the human spirit and how easily it can become tangled up in itself and become embarrassed. I assure you that, as you reflect on this, you will more easily understand what I have so often told you: The inner torments you have endured and still feel traces of occurred because of a multitude of thoughts and desires produced by a great eagerness to attain an imaginary perfection that was actually a distortion. Your imagination formed an idea of the absolute perfection you wanted to attain, but what happened? You know very well. Your will, fearful of the great difficulty and impossibility involved, remained pregnant without being able to bring to birth, causing many desires to multiply like huge flies that eat the honey from the honeycomb while your good and genuine desires were starving for consolation. It is a good thing that God had compassion on your soul and freed you from this.

(To Luigi Bozzutto, November 25, 1917)

May 15

The virtue of patience is the one that assures us of perfection more than any of the other virtues. Although you need to practice it with others, you also need to practice it with yourself. Those who aspire to a pure love of God actually need patience not so much with others but with themselves. To acquire perfection, you need to put up with your own imperfections. I tell you to tolerate them patiently, but that does not mean you should cherish them or be fond of them. Humility is nourished through this suffering. My dearest son, to move ahead in a good way, you need to apply yourself diligently to walk the path that is right in front of you, the path on which you can go forward and make good progress from the very first day.

… Our imperfections, my son, will be with us until we die; we cannot walk without touching the ground. It is true, however, that just as you should not consider halting or turning back on your path, so too you should not think about flying, because we are like small chicks that have not yet grown any wings.

(To Luigi Bozzutto, November 25, 1917)

May 16

Our earthly life is perishing little by little, and we need to have our imperfections die the same way. Imperfections, for pious souls who endure them, can be sources of merit and powerful motivators to acquire virtue, because these imperfections help us to see the depth of our spiritual poverty and move us to exercise humility.

… All that I have written you, my son, was written at the feet of the Crucified One. I had a heartfelt impulse to write all this to you, because I think most of your painful times in the past were caused by having put forth great effort but seeing minimal results. When you were not strong enough to put your ideas into practice, you were tormented by heartbreak and frustration, by disturbances in your mind and heart. If this is true, and unfortunately it probably is, be careful in the future to be more down to earth, because sailing on the high seas can lead you to capsize and result in shipwreck.

(To Luigi Bozzutto, November 25, 1917)

May 17

I advise a holy simplicity that captures the heart of Jesus because it is appropriate for this stage of your life. Do not fear the dangers you see far ahead that you have written to me about and have spoken about at great length many times….

Have a firm overall intention, my son, to want to serve and love God with all your heart, and beyond that do not take thought for the future. Just think about doing good today, and when tomorrow comes, it will be called today, and then you can think about it.

Always have trust and surrender to Divine Providence, and do not insist on provision for more manna than you need for today. Have no doubt that God will rain down more manna tomorrow and will do so all the days of your life.

(To Luigi Bozzutto, November 25, 1917)

May 18

What is most important to the holy apostle is love, so he recommends it more than any other virtue. He wants it to be part of every action, since it is the one and only virtue that constitutes Christian perfection: "And over all these [other virtues]," he says, "put on love, which binds everything together in perfect harmony" [Colossians 3:14].

Look, he is not satisfied with recommending patience and mutual support of one another, which are also noble virtues. No, he highlights love, and for good reason, since it is very possible that a person could patiently forbear the imperfections of others and forgive any offenses received, but all of this is without merit if it is done without love, which is the queen of virtues and encloses within itself all the other virtues.

(To Raffaelina Cerase, November 16, 1914)

May 19

Among the many ways to achieve Christian perfection, the apostle proposes two powerful ones: the continuous study of God's law and doing everything for his glory.

Concerning the first, he writes to the Colossians, "Let the word of Christ dwell in you richly, as you teach and admonish one another in all wisdom, and as you sing psalms and hymns and spiritual songs with thankfulness in your hearts to God" [Colossians 3:16]....

The apostle wants the law of God, the word of Christ, to dwell in us abundantly. This cannot happen if we do not diligently read sacred Scripture and books that deal with the things of God or if we do not hear God's word through sermons, in the confessional, and so on....

Concerning doing all for the glory of God, let us hear the apostle's teaching: "Whatever you do, in word or deed, do everything in the name of the Lord Jesus, giving thanks to God the Father through him" [Colossians 3:17].

By faithfully practicing this simple method, not only will we keep ourselves from every sin, but we will also be spurred on at every moment to go forward to greater perfection at all times.

(To Raffaelina Cerase, November 16, 1914)

May 20

I do not have adequate words or feelings to thank the goodness of the Lord, who so lovingly deals with you and protects you. I clearly see, my good daughter, he has chosen you to be close to him, though not because of any of your own merits. By now you can be sure that he wants to possess your heart completely and wants it to be pierced with sorrow and love like his. Illness, heart pangs, caresses, holy flames that consume us, temptations, dryness, and desolation are all various features of his ineffable love. When the evil one wants to convince you that you are a casualty of his attacks and a victim of divine abandonment, do not believe him, because he is lying and wants to deceive you.

It is not true that you are sinning; it is not true that you disgust the Lord; it is not true that the Lord has not forgiven your transgressions and wandering in the past.

God's grace is with you, and you are very precious to the Lord. The shadows, the fears, the contradictory perspectives are all devilish tricks that you must reject in the holy name of obedience.

(To Girolama Longo, April 15, 1918)

May 21

Give free course to your tears, because that is the work of God in you, and do not be concerned about what bystanders might think. The stabs of pain that you experience in your heart are willed by God, and he wills them because his mercy makes you precious to him, and he wants you to resemble his beloved Son in his suffering in the desert, in the garden, and on the cross....

The one counsel I would give you is to cling firmly to what I told you in the Lord, and do not allow anything to be in you except what the Holy Spirit longs to do in you. Abandon yourself to his will for you, and do not be afraid. He is so subtle, wise, and gentle that he will not bring about anything but good.

Do not be wary of inner delights, especially when they are accompanied by a profound sense of humility, so open wide your heart to receive them.

(To Girolama Longo, April 15, 1918)

May 22

Join your heart to Jesus' heart, and be simple of heart the way he wants you to be. Try to reflect the simplicity of Jesus in your life, keeping worldly wisdom and sophistication far from your heart. Try to have a mind that is always pure in its thoughts, always righteous in its ideas, always holy in its intentions. Try to have a will that seeks nothing but God and his preferences and seeks glory and honor only from him.

Let us mirror Jesus, my dear, in his hidden life. All of his infinite majesty was hidden in the shadows and in the silence of that humble workshop in Nazareth. Therefore let us also try to lead an inner life that is hidden in God.

(To Raffaelina Cerase, July 14, 1914)

May 23

Do not be dismayed about the cross. The surest proof of love occurs when someone suffers for the beloved. If God suffered so much pain because he loved us so much, then the pain we suffer for his sake becomes pleasant because we love him. In the afflictions the Lord gives you as gifts, be patient and conform yourself to the divine heart with joy, knowing that it is all a continual game on the part of the Lover.

Tribulations, crosses, have always been the inheritance and portion of elect souls. To the extent that Jesus wants to raise a soul to perfection, he then increases the cross of tribulation. Rejoice, I tell you, to see yourself so privileged despite your lack of merit. The more you are afflicted, the more you should exult, because a soul in the fire of tribulation will become refined gold, worthy to shine in the kingdom of heaven.

(To Raffaelina Cerase, July 14, 1914)

May 24

That miserable devil is redoubling his efforts to harm me. However, I fear nothing except offending God. It seems to me that the evil one is more concerned about you than he is about me, because he wants to deprive me of your guidance. In fact, it does take much effort for me to communicate about my situation: I have such severe pain in my head that I almost cannot see where to put the pen down on the paper.

All the wicked fantasies the devil has been putting into my mind vanish when I confidently abandon myself into Jesus' arms. Therefore, if I am crucified with Christ, that is, if I meditate on his afflictions, I suffer immensely, but it is a sorrow that does me much good. I enjoy a peace and tranquillity that cannot be described.

(To Fr. Benedetto of San Marco in Lamis, April 29, 1911)

May 25

Before uniting myself to Jesus in the morning through the Eucharist, my heart feels drawn by a power from above. I have such a hunger and thirst for him before receiving him that I am almost breathless....

However, as soon as I am satisfied after I receive him in the Eucharist, my hunger and thirst grow even more intense. After I am already in possession of the Highest Good, then at that very moment the fullness of sweetness becomes so great that I almost have to say to Jesus, "Enough! I cannot bear it anymore." I almost forget that I am still on earth, and my mind and heart desire nothing more.

(To Fr. Benedetto of San Marco in Lamis, April 29, 1911)

May 26

In these very sad times when so many people are falling away from God, I cannot understand how anyone can live a genuine life without spiritual food for strength. In these times when we are continually surrounded by people who hate God in their hearts and always have blasphemy on their lips, the sure way to keep ourselves free from the stench of the pestilence that surrounds us is to fortify ourselves with eucharistic food.

Keeping free from sin and making progress on the path of perfection cannot be achieved today by anyone who lives for months at a time without feasting on the spotless flesh of the Lamb of God. I do not know what other people think about this issue. However, I have always believed that, given the actual circumstances in which we live, it is an illusion for people to think that they are taking any steps toward perfection when they limit themselves to taking Communion once or twice a year.

(To Raffaelina Cerase, May 19, 1914)

May 27

My sister, we need to hold this virtue [charity] in highest esteem if we want to obtain mercy from the heavenly Father. Let us esteem it highly and practice it; it is the virtue that makes us all sons and daughters of the one Father who is in heaven. Let us love and practice this virtue, since it is the divine Master's primary commandment. Loving and practicing charity is what distinguishes us from other people. Let us love charity and flee any shadow that can obscure it in any way. Yes, let us love charity and always keep in mind the great teaching of the apostle that "you are the body of Christ and individually members of it" [1 Corinthians 12:27] and that Jesus is the only head of his members. Let us love one another and remember that we are all called to form one single body. If we preserve charity among ourselves, the wonderful peace of Jesus will triumph more and more in our hearts.

(To Raffaelina Cerase, November 16, 1914)

May 28

You know, dear daughter, the remedy I heartily recommend is tranquillity of spirit, and I always forbid excessive worry. You must seek to restore your spirit to a state of rest and tranquillity after having been agitated by the work of the evil one. Do this by thinking of the spiritual rest that our souls should always have in God's will, wherever his will leads us. My daughter, live in this valley of tears for as long as it pleases God, with total submission to his holy will. We are very much indebted to divine goodness for making us so fervently desire to live and die according to his pleasure. My daughter, let us trust that our great Savior, who gives us the intention to live and die in our enjoyment of him, will give us the grace to live that way.

(To Annita Rodote, May 28, 1917)

May 29

Always keep in mind this meaningful lesson that is worthy of being well understood: This present life is given to us only so that we may acquire the eternal one. The failure to understand this leads us to set our affections on things of this world that we are passing through, and when it is time for us to leave it, we become terrified and upset. Believe me, my dear schoolteacher, in order to be content during our pilgrimage, we need to keep before us the hope of reaching that home where we will live eternally, and in the meantime we need to be steadfast in our faith. Since God has called us to himself, he is concerned about our journey to him, so he will never allow anything to happen to us that is not for our greater good. He knows what we are, so he will stretch out his fatherly hand when we falter so that nothing can hold us back from running swiftly to him. However, in order to fully enjoy this grace, we need to have complete trust in him.

(To Erminia Gargani, April 23, 1918)

May 30

Tell me, is it the sun or the darkness that illuminates and reveals objects? I leave it to you to draw out the correct implications here. God alone gives grace. God alone is the supreme sun, and all the other so-called suns either are worthless or derive from him. God alone, I tell you, can illumine a soul through his grace and reveal its condition. The more a soul understands its poverty and unworthiness before God, the more pronounced is the grace that revealed this self-knowledge.

I understand that the discovery of one's spiritual poverty through the activity of this divine sun is a reason at first for sadness and sorrow, pain and terror, for any poor soul that becomes enlightened this way. However, comfort yourself in our sweetest Lord, because when this divine sun will have warmed the earth of your spirit with its burning rays, it will cause new plants to burst forth that will, in time, yield exquisite fruit—fruit never seen before.

(To Raffaelina Cerase, March 4, 1915)

May 31

Jesus is always with you, even when it seems you do not feel him. He is never closer to you than when you are in spiritual battle. He is always there, near you, invigorating you to keep up the battle courageously; he is there to fend off the blows of the enemy so that you are not harmed.

For the sake of love, I implore you, by all that you hold most sacred, do not wrong him by suspecting, even slightly, that you have been abandoned by him—not even for a single instant. This is precisely one of the most satanic temptations, and you need to thrust it far from you as soon as you become aware of it.

Be consoled, my dear, that the days of humiliation and unhappy years we can count in our present life will be far outweighed by the profound and intimate joys of eternity. This is not just my way of seeing and thinking, because sacred Scripture gives us this infallible testimony. Here is what the psalmist says about it: "Make us glad as many days as you have afflicted us, / and as many years as we have seen evil" [Psalm 90:15]. And the apostle Paul wrote in a letter he sent to the Corinthians, "This slight momentary affliction is preparing us for an eternal weight of glory beyond all comparison" [2 Corinthians 4:17].

(To Raffaelina Cerase, August 15, 1914)

JUNE

June 1

Yes, let us do good works. Now is the time to plant seeds. If we want to gather much fruit, we do not necessarily need to plant many seeds; what we need is to scatter those seeds on good soil. We have already sown many seeds, but that is still not enough if we want to rejoice during the time of harvest. Let us spread still more seed around, my dear, but do not be grieved about having to do that. Let us try to have the seed fall on good soil, and when the heat comes to open up the seed and make it a plant, then let us be vigilant to take care that the tares do not come and suffocate the tender young plants.

(To Raffaelina Cerase, December 10, 1914)

June 2

Oh my father! Do not leave me alone. Help me with your prayers and with your insights. I tell you I feel such loneliness that it takes away my calm and rest and even my appetite. If things keep up this way, I am on the brink of a great crisis, because I know that the physical side of life is subject to things that happen in one's spirit. I am more fearful of unhealthy physical reactions not for my sake but solely and entirely for the sake of others.

(To Fr. Benedetto of San Marco in Lamis, October 8, 1920)

June 3

For some time now my soul finds itself immersed day and night in the dark night of the soul. This spiritual darkness lasts for many long hours, for many long days, and often for whole weeks....

But God is alive! The thought of immortality, which resists hell itself, presents itself soon after to my bewildered soul that is about to lose heart. My soul senses that it is still in a living body and is about to ask for help from others,...but at that point my tongue becomes mute, and it is not worth saying what is happening to me then.

I am floundering around. I sigh, I weep, I lament, but all in vain. Finally, exhausted from pain and completely helpless, my poor soul submits to the Lord and says, "Not my will, sweet Jesus, but yours be done."

(To Fr. Agostino of San Marco in Lamis, end of January, 1916)

June 4

My God! I am bewildered and have lost you. Will I ever find you again, or have I lost you forever? Have you condemned me to live eternally far away from your face?...

My father, I am doing what I can in this darkened prison, but it is arduous to advance through the dark forest of these thick shadows, through the tempest and the harassment of the enemy, who takes advantage of all this to try to make me transgress and to conquer me.

I look for God, but where can I find him? Every idea of him as Lord, God, Master, Creator, Lover, Life fades away.... In vain I revisit disconnected memories and a love that I lost, and I am no longer able to love. Oh my Good, where are you to be found? I have lost you, and I am bewildered in trying to track you down.

(To Fr. Benedetto of San Marco in Lamis, June 4, 1918)

June 5

I bow my head, I bow it again willingly, to the blows of the divine justice that is rightfully indignant with me. But nothing works anymore to reawaken eternal life in me, nothing works anymore to reanimate my mortally wounded spirit....

Praying, my father, brings a sting of mortal pain and suffering now that is terrible to recall. I cannot piece anything together. I do not know if my prayers are really prayers or just expressions of strong resentment that my heart addresses to God out of the fullness of my pain. I feel an empty void within me that is horrible to think about when I am in that state. God is always hidden to my spirit, although I watch for him and am being worn down in my frantic but necessary quest.

(To Fr. Benedetto of San Marco in Lamis, June 4, 1918)

June 6

My very dear father, do not abandon me in this anguish. I am on the brink of losing myself. I am about to be crushed under the heavy hand of a God who is justly indignant with me. Remember that the Lord entrusted me to you for guidance, comfort, and salvation. Remember that from the very moment that the Lord entrusted me to you, I considered you the father of my soul, and I promised heaven all the tenderness of a son for you, which I have felt and still nourish. I always followed your assurances and teachings with great eagerness.

Oh my father! Help me! If it were possible, I would completely pour out my languishing soul in this very letter, but you know that is not possible for me because I am painfully incapacitated.... All I can do is cry out, and that should make you understand my poverty, my lowliness, my misery, my neediness. Implore heaven on my behalf for help, for my perfect accommodation to the hidden divine and holy wishes, for steadfast docility, and for constant and resolute obedience—the only wooden plank to help me through the crashing storms, the only plank that I can cling to in this spiritual shipwreck.

(To Fr. Benedetto of San Marco in Lamis, June 4, 1918)

June 7

While undergoing such severity from you, Most High, I declare myself a most obedient son to my guide. I beg you to give me strength for my suffering, since I am stripped of every comfort from you. In addition, make my resolutions constant, steadfast, and fruitful, at least enough so that they are sufficient to disarm your fury. Offer these resolutions to your offended majesty yourself, my Highest Good, but not before undergirding them by your divine power. Meanwhile I will attempt to find a posture for my unbearable pain on this bed of sharp and cruel thorns, receiving your rejection of me as my only food.

Do not think, my father, that I have not done everything I could to come out of this harsh prison, but it has all been useless. Trying to do so was to my detriment, because I should have just resigned myself to the darkness descending into my soul and entered even more into the thick of the fight. My crying out was in vain.

(To Fr. Benedetto of San Marco in Lamis, June 4, 1918)

June 8

I am lost, yes, lost, in the unknown. I am stripped of everything. Nevertheless, I am resolved, despite feeling no comfort, to follow only the voice of the one who is standing in for God. I hunger for God to return to my soul; give him back to me, feed him to me, the one who is my life and my all. My spirit is in total collapse, with only sinister lights that tend to illuminate my breakdown and cause dismay to this victim, a prey to his unknown destiny. My God! I have to cry out, my father, because that is all that is left to me in my intense pain. I understand nothing at all, and I very much fear being abandoned forever to myself, and in that fear I clutch at, or dare to clutch at, obedience, but that seems to elude me....

Bless me always, and I in return will never stop sacrificing myself on your behalf to this God that I have lost.

(To Fr. Benedetto of San Marco in Lamis, June 4, 1918)

June 9

I find myself in extreme desolation. I am alone in carrying the weight of everything. The thought of not being able to bring spiritual comfort to those whom Jesus sends me, the thought of seeing so many souls who dizzy themselves to justify their wrongdoing in defiance of the Highest Good, afflicts me, torments me, almost kills me. It overwhelms my mind and tears my heart apart.

Oh God! What thorns are piercing my heart! The two desires that seem extremely contrary that are pulling on me—wanting to live to benefit my brethren in exile here on earth and wanting to die to unite myself to my Bridegroom—have recently become magnified to a superlative degree in the deepest part of my spirit. They are tearing my soul apart and taking away my peace—not the deep inner peace of my soul but the peace that is on the outside, so to speak. However, that peace is very necessary for me to be able to act with more gentleness and more anointing.

(To Fr. Benedetto of San Marco in Lamis, October 8, 1920)

June 10

How can I tell you about the intense torment that is making a martyr of my soul? Since Thursday my soul has more than ever been filled with extreme turmoil. I feel the hand of the Lord pressing down on me. I feel the Lord demonstrating all his power to punish me, and I am being rejected like a wind-tossed leaf and persecuted.

Oh! I can no longer withstand it! I can no longer endure the weight of his justice. I feel myself crushed under his mighty hand. My tears are my daily food. I am agitated and I seek him, but I find him only in the furor of his justice.

Oh my father, I can quite rightly say with the psalmist that I have come to deep waters and the flood has submerged me. I cry out and wear myself out in vain…. Fear and trembling have come upon me, and I am completely covered by darkness. I am stretched out on my bed of sorrows, and I am frantically seeking my God. Where is he?

(To Fr. Benedetto of San Marco in Lamis, June 4, 1918)

June 11

There are certain physical afflictions that can be cured by changing our lifestyle. However, self-love, an inflated estimation of ourselves, and a false freedom of spirit are roots that cannot be easily eradicated from the human heart. We can impede the production of their fruit, that is, sins. However, their first buds and entwining branches—their first appearance and initial movements—cannot in fact be avoided as long as we are in this mortal life. Nevertheless, we can moderate and diminish their strength and quality by practicing the contrary virtues, especially love for God.

You need to have patience, then, to break off bad habits, to dominate aversions, and to overcome your own inclinations and moods that occur in some circumstances, because, my good daughter, this life is a continual battle, and no one can say, "I am not being attacked." The life of calm is reserved for heaven.

(To Erminia Gargani, June 11, 1918)

June 12

My daughter, charity has three facets: love of God, affection for oneself, and preference for one's neighbor. My simple teaching here will help you start to practice these.

(a) Often throughout the day, give your whole heart, soul, and mind to God with great confidence, and tell him, along with the royal prophet, "I am yours, save me" [Psalm 119:94]. Do not stop to consider what kind of prayer God is giving you, but simply and humbly go along with his grace concerning the affection you should have for yourself.

(b) Be attentive to eradicate evil tendencies but without excessively wearing yourself out. Do not be surprised at finding yourself wretched and full of bad moods. Look after your heart with a great desire to perfect it.

(To Erminia Gargani, June 11, 1918)

June 13

(c) Be good to your neighbors, and do not allow yourself outbursts of anger. Repeat these concepts from the Master very often in your daily life: "I have loved these neighbors, eternal Father, because you love them. You have given them to me as brothers and sisters, and I want to love them the way you love them." In particular love these young girls, your disciples, the ones to whom the very hand of Divine Providence has linked you and with whom you have a heavenly bond. Do not be concerned about the outbursts of impatience that you are used to having, because there is no guilt in these unless they are premeditated.

(To Erminia Gargani, June 11, 1918)

June 14

Charity's sisters are joy and peace. Joy comes from the enjoyment of possessing what we love. From the moment that the soul knows God, it is naturally motivated to love him. If the soul follows this natural impulse as it is stirred up by the Holy Spirit, it is already loving the Supreme Good. This blessed soul already possesses the beautiful virtue of charity. Now, in loving God, the soul is already sure of possessing him, because, unlike people who love money, honors, and good health but do not yet have what they love, the one who loves God has the object it loves at once.

This idea does not come from me but from sacred Scripture, which tells us, "He who abides in love abides in God, and God abides in him" [1 John 4:16].

(To Raffaelina Cerase, October 23, 1914)

June 15

Joy is the offspring of charity. But to be perfect and genuine, joy requires peace as its inseparable companion. Peace is produced in us when the good that we have is in fact the highest good and is assured to us. Now, isn't God the highest good that the soul loves, and in loving him, doesn't the soul possess him?

In addition to being the highest good, the good that we possess needs to be securely ours. Now, the divine Master assures us, "No one will take your joy from you" [John 16:22]. What more solid testimony can there be than that? Realizing all this, the soul cannot help but feel completely content. This is what makes a person able to face the most bitter contradictions of life with a cheerful heart.

(To Raffaelina Cerase, October 23, 1914)

June 16

I must note that as long as the soul is in the state of pilgrimage, it will never reach perfect charity, and therefore its peace can never be perfected either. Life's many contradictions, tribulations, and conflicts that burden the poor soul are numerous; the soul can experience such agony at certain times in life that life itself can become unbearable. That can happen when a soul feels in danger of complete ruin.

Now, to resist such harsh trials, patience is necessary; it is the virtue that makes us bear every adversity without giving up…. It is through this virtue that the soul remains integrated internally.

(To Raffaelina Cerase, October 23, 1914)

June 17

Charity, joy, and peace are the virtues that perfect the soul concerning what it already possesses, while patience perfects the soul concerning the things it must endure.

These four virtues are for the interior perfection of the soul. However, for external perfection the soul needs a variety of virtues, some of which concern our behavior toward our neighbor and some of which concern the disciplining of our senses.

As for the virtues that the soul needs in connection to our neighbor, kindness is paramount, by means of which a devout soul is characterized as being pleasant, courteous, civil, and averse to every kind of rudeness. That soul thus draws others by these qualities to an imitation of the devout life.

(To Raffaelina Cerase, October 23, 1914)

June 18

There are three virtues that perfect the devout person in terms of disciplining the senses: modesty, continence, and chastity. Through modesty a devout soul succeeds in ruling over all its external actions. St. Paul was quite right to recommend this virtue to everyone and to claim that it was necessary. On top of that, Paul wants that virtue to be seen by others. Through continence the soul succeeds in keeping the senses of sight, touch, taste, smell, and hearing away from excessive pleasures, even permissible ones. With chastity, the virtue that transforms our nature into an angelic one, the soul keeps sensuality in check and turns it away from pleasures that are forbidden.

There you have the noblest picture of Christian perfection. Blessed is the soul that possesses these virtues, all of which are fruits of the Holy Spirit who indwells it. That soul has nothing to fear. It will shine forth in the world like the sun in the midst of the firmament.

(To Raffaelina Cerase, October 23, 1914)

June 19

Where can I find my God? Where can I find rest for my poor heart, which feels as though it were being ripped out of my chest? I am seeking him faithfully, but I do not find him. I knock at the heart of the divine prison keeper, but he does not answer me. What does all this mean? Has my lack of faithfulness made him so inflexible? Can I hope for mercy that he will finally hear my cries, or should I renounce that hope? Oh God! May my horrid obstinacy be finally shattered. My God! May I love you at last with the kind of love you require. May I return to you at last from this painful and heartbreaking search.

My father, my spirit is stripped and bleak; my heart is dry and parched and inclined toward my God. My spirit and heart make hardly any movement toward the one who created them out of his bounty. I have almost no faith left; I am incapable of lifting myself up on the merciful wings of hope—the virtue so necessary during abandonment by God, when the height of the storm is raging and an overflowing measure of misery crushes me; I have no love left.

(To Fr. Benedetto of San Marco in Lamis, June 19, 1918)

June 20

Yes, I am stripped of everything, my father, even of every trace of virtue, to the point that it seems I am in a deadly state of lukewarmness for which God is justly rejecting me. And I see that my ruin is irreparable, because I see no way out of this. Alas! I have lost every path, every means, every support, every guideline. And if I try to stir up my dull memory, a mysterious mental chaos occurs, and I find myself more lost than before, more incapable of getting up again, and the mysterious darkness becomes denser.

My God, why do you shake, prick, reawaken, and cause dismay to this dejected soul, this soul that is already devastated with a ruin that you have said is accomplished, caused, and willed by your very command and permission?

(To Fr. Benedetto of San Marco in Lamis, June 19, 1918)

June 21

Oh my father! Tell me what you know about him, I beseech you. Do not reproach me for my scattered state, my anxiety, my wandering in search of him. Do not reproach me for the distress of my spirit that is longing for its humble and unseen place of repose in divine approbation. Tell me, please, where is my God? How can I find him? What should I be doing to seek him? Tell me, will I find him? Tell me, where should I entrust this heart that is sick unto death and that is by instinct always engaged in a continually frantic and painful search?

Oh God, oh God! I cannot say anything else. Why have you abandoned me? My spirit, justly shaken by your divine justice, is tied up in knots without any resources or insight except for fleeting flashes of light that exacerbate my pain and martyrdom.

(To Fr. Benedetto of San Marco in Lamis, June 19, 1918)

June 22

Be patient yet a little longer in bearing your spiritual desolation. Be patient in enduring the loving trials that Jesus, who wants to make you like him, is making you undergo in his wonderful providence. You will see the Lord one day completely answer your prayers, which are also mine. Do not be dismayed if the night within you becomes deeper and gloomier. Do not be afraid if your physical eyes do not see the calm heaven that envelops your soul, but look up. Lift your eyes up above yourself, and you will see a shining light that participates in the light of the eternal sun.

Lively faith, confident belief, and complete adherence to the authority God has placed over you—this constitutes the light that illuminated the path for the people of God in the desert. It is the light that always shines in the deepest recesses of every spirit accepted by the Father. It is the light that led the magi to the adoration of the newly born Messiah, the star prophesied by Balaam [see Number 24:17], the torchlight that directs the steps of souls in desolation. This light, this star, and this torch are what illuminate your soul and direct your steps so that you do not falter.… Be assured and believe that this sun shines in your soul, and it is the very sun that the prophet of God sang about: "In your light do we see light" [Psalm 36:9].

(To Assunta di Tomaso, October 22, 1916)

June 23

Do not be discouraged if your trial is always increasing. Believe at all times, lift your heart up on high, and you can be certain that there is no reason for dismay. Trials are hard; everyone knows that. So what, then? Isn't it God who is overseeing everything and ordering everything for our greater good? Therefore be strong in the day of trial. Wait a bit longer, and our good God will hear our prayer. Hasn't he heard so many prayers up to this point? Therefore he cannot fail to hear this last one, the crown of all prayers.

Wait a bit longer! Do we know how long "a bit longer" is? It does not matter, my good daughter! You will see the answer when it pleases the divine Bridegroom and when we are all transformed in him. You will most definitely experience his promise, *Videbitis me*—"You will see me" [see Matthew 26:64].

(To Assunta di Tomaso, October 22, 1916)

June 24

The stabs of pain and expansions of soul that alternate in the deepest part of your spirit come from a love that pushes us away and then draws us back. Therefore be at peace, and calmly endure these alternations of diverse feelings in your spirit. They are due to your incomplete possession of the object of love and are causing the internal martyrdom that makes your soul suffer severely. Endure them so that you can say with the royal prophet, "Behold, it was for my welfare / that I had great bitterness" [Isaiah 38:17]. Open up your soul to the eternal sun, and do not fear its burning, fiery rays. Open up your soul, I tell you, most beloved daughters of my heart, to this sun of infinite beauty—you who are longing so much for the cocoon to hatch so that the lovely butterfly can be released from its harsh, dark prison.

(To the Campanile sisters, May 25, 1918)

June 25

The high-society Christian esteems honors, riches, conceit, comforts, and all the things this very vile world can offer. Fool! Retreat into yourself, and remember that through your baptism you renounced the world and that you are dead to it. The Holy Spirit tells you this through the mouth of Paul: "You have died, and your life is hidden with Christ in God" [Colossians 3:3].

Remember, foolish one, that the life of someone who lives in the Spirit of Jesus will not always remain hidden and unknown. Remember what will happen in the day of the Lord: "When Christ who is our life appears, then you also will appear with him in glory" [Colossians 3:4]. To comfort the faithful, the beloved apostle St. John wrote, "Beloved, we are God's children now; it does not yet appear what we shall be, but we know that when he appears we shall be like him, for we shall see him as he is" [1 John 3:2].

Isn't the assurance of such boundless glory, foolish man, enough to make you recollect yourself, come to your senses, and follow your vocation as a Christian for the rest of your days?

(To Raffaelina Cerase, November 16, 1914)

June 26

The souls that are most afflicted are the favorites of the divine heart, and you can be sure that Jesus has chosen you to be the darling of his adorable heart.

You must hide yourself in this heart. You must pour out your desires into this heart. Live whatever days providence allots you within this heart. Die in this heart at the time it pleases the Lord. I have placed you in this heart, for it is within this heart that you live and move and have your being.

(To the Campanile sisters, May 31, 1918)

June 27

How happy is the kingdom within us when his holy love rules it! How blessed are the faculties of the soul when it obeys such a wise King! No, dearest father, Love does not allow any grave sin or the least affection for the most minor of sins to dwell in this kingdom under his governance.

It is true that Love allows sin to approach the borders of the soul so that it can develop the internal virtues to wage war and be strengthened. And it is also true that he allows spies, those venial sins and imperfections, to run here and there within his kingdom. However, this is permitted only in order to make us know that apart from him we would be a prey to our enemies.

(To Fr. Benedetto of San Marco in Lamis, July 23, 1917)

June 28

No one should ever regret time spent for the glory of God and for the salvation of souls, because it is never time badly spent. Therefore do not worry about robbing me of my time, as I already told you earlier. Time spent in obtaining health and sanctification for the souls of others is indeed time well spent. I have no way to thank the goodness of the heavenly Father when he sends me souls that I can help in some way.

Oh, would that it had pleased heaven for me to have spent all the days of my life in this holy ministry!

(To Raffaelina Cerase, May 31, 1914)

June 29

"Wretched man that I am!" exclaimed the great chosen vessel, the Apostle to the Gentiles. "Who will deliver me from this body of death?" [Romans 7:24]. There can be no doubt that this apostle was one of the greatest saints and a star of the first magnitude in our holy church. How many persecutions, toils, and pains he suffered for Jesus Christ! What burning charity, what fiery love, what ardent zeal for Jesus' honor! What revelations, visions, ecstasies, and raptures even into the third heaven! And yet this holy apostle, rich in so many virtues and with such excellent gifts, expressed the lament above.... [He tells us,] "Three times I have been beaten with rods; once I was stoned. Three times I have been shipwrecked; a night and a day I have been adrift at sea" [2 Corinthians 11:25]. He also speaks of other hardships he endured out of love for Jesus: "many a sleepless night, in hunger and thirst, often without food, in cold and exposure" [2 Corinthians 11:27]....

Tell me, daughter, is there anything lacking that prevents us from declaring this great apostle and teacher of the gentiles perfect? Yet even he felt in himself a whole host of moods, aversions, and natural habits and inclinations that were conspiring to his undoing and to spiritual death.... He answers that dilemma quoted above by saying that the grace of God through Jesus Christ will keep him not from fear or terror or battle—all the things you are feeling, my dear daughter—but from being overcome and conquered.

(To Maria Gargani, June 18, 1917)

June 30

Always remain in the presence of God in the ways you have been and will be taught. Keep yourself from anxiety and disquiet, because nothing will prevent you more than these things from walking in the path of perfection. Gently place your heart in the wounds of Our Lord…. Have great confidence in his mercy and goodness that he will never abandon you, but do not neglect embracing his cross because of that confidence.

After your love for Our Lord, I recommend that you love the church, his spouse and our tender mother…. Thank God a hundred times a day for being a daughter of the church…. Have compassion for all the church's pastors and preachers, as well as for all the guardians of souls; see, my daughter, how they are spread out across the face of the earth…. Pray to God for them, that as they work out their own salvation, they may fruitfully procure the salvation of souls. As you do this, I ask you not to forget me when you find yourself before Jesus, just as he has never let me forget you.

(To Antonietta Vona, January 16, 1918)

JULY

July 1

After the battle there comes a crown, and the more conflicts the soul has, the more victory palms there will be. Knowing that there is a new level of eternal glory for every victory won, why then, my very beloved daughter, are you not rejoicing that you are engaged in winning so many battles in the course of your life? Let this thought comfort you, and let the example of our divine Master spur you on, for he was "one who in every respect has been tempted as we are, yet without sinning" [Hebrews 4:15], and he was tempted to the point of exclaiming, "My God, my God, why have you forsaken me?" [Matthew 27:46].

Do not listen to or believe the enemy when he tells you that God has rejected you or that God is punishing you for some hidden unfaithfulness and is wanting to chastise you to remove it from your soul. That is *not the least bit true.* When a soul grieves and fears offending God, it does not offend him and is far from doing so.

(To Margherita Tresca, May 17, 1918)

July 2

The one who is agitating and tormenting you is Satan; the one who enlightens and consoles you is God. The soul that is led to abase and humble itself more and more before the Lord and at the same time is eager to suffer and endure everything to gain the approval of the heavenly Bridegroom must recognize that this leading comes from God's providence. The ardent longings of a soul for more love for the Lord are not, and cannot be, delusions or illusions. Therefore I assure you that the grace of Jesus is the source of whatever good things are taking place in you. Therefore allow the divine Bridegroom to work in you and lead you on the paths he chooses.

(To Raffaelina Cerase, July 14, 1914)

July 3

Do not yield yourself to Satan's tempests, and let your confidence always rest in God. Increase your trust at all times, especially now in this current trial that will give glory to God and be a great triumph for your soul. Do not be unnecessarily distressed. Rejoice, for the war will not delay in coming to an end. Accounts will soon be tallied, and the costs of the war will be levied against God's enemy, the enemy of souls. Oh, how lovely it will be on the day when our good God will shine forth after your purging! May this sweet thought, then, reinvigorate you to fight the good fight valiantly.

(To Raffaelina Cerase, March 25, 1915)

July 4

In your state of affliction, continue to pray for everyone, especially for the exaltation of our Holy Mother Church; pray for poor sinners in order to compensate for the many offenses that are committed against the Sacred Heart.

I know that you have sacrificed yourself and are still sacrificing yourself continually to the Lord. Jesus has accepted your sacrifice; he has given you the grace to bear the sacrifice. Have courage for a little while longer then, because your reward is not far off.

Do not be afraid when you experience darkness and dryness of spirit, because there is no reason to fear. Your current or past infidelities are not the reason for the current state of your soul. *Believe me* because I am not deceiving you.

Do not stop doing what you normally do, and be assured that Jesus is satisfied with that. Your soul is moving forward without your realizing it or understanding it.

(To Annita Rodote, June 4, 1918)

July 5

You are mistaken, greatly mistaken, in wanting to measure the love a soul has for its Creator by the palpable sweetness it feels in loving God. That kind of experience belongs to souls who are still in the simplicity of their spiritual infancy. It is the kind of love that could be fatal for a soul who gives itself over too much to that. Instead, the love of souls who have grown beyond their spiritual infancy is a love that loves without receiving enjoyment and sweetness in that part of themselves that is called the sensible soul.

The sure sign that a soul genuinely loves God is that it is always ready to observe God's holy laws; it is always attentive and vigilant to avoid falling into sin. That soul has a habitual desire to see the heavenly Father glorified and to that end overlooks nothing within its power to spread the kingdom of God. That soul always prays to the divine Father with the same words the divine Master used: "Father,... Your kingdom come" [Luke 11:2].

(To Raffaelina Cerase, December 29, 1914)

July 6

You need to hold fast to two virtues: kindness toward your neighbor and humility toward God.

I trust that you will do this, because that great God who has taken you by the hand to draw you to himself will not abandon you until he brings you into his eternal tabernacle. It is fitting, my dearest daughters, that you put all your effort into eradicating any pretensions and thoughts of preeminence, because honor is never more attained than when it is despised. A desire for honor can disquiet the soul and lead to omissions and errors contrary to kindness and humility.

(To the Campanile sisters, October 18, 1917)

July 7

This morning after Mass, while I was quite sad about a hundred matters, all of a sudden I got such a violent headache that at first it seemed impossible for me to continue giving thanks.

That only increased my torment, and a great dryness of spirit came over me. Who knows what might have happened if what I am about to tell you had not occurred? Our Lord appeared to me and said, "My son, write down what you hear from me today so that you do not forget it. I am faithful, and no creature will be lost without knowing it. Light is very different from darkness. When I speak to a soul, I always draw it to myself. When the enemy speaks, that tends to distance a soul from me. The fear I inspire in a soul never makes it pull away from me. The devil, on the other hand, never puts fear in a soul to bring it closer to me.

"The fears that a soul can feel at certain times in life about its eternal salvation, if they come from me, can be recognized by the peace and serenity they bring."

This vision of Our Lord and what he said have flooded my soul with such peace and contentment that all the sweetest things this world can offer seem insipid by comparison to the single pearl of this blessedness.

(To Fr. Benedetto of San Marco in Lamis, July 7, 1913)

July 8

It seems to me that Jesus is always looking at me. If I sometimes lose God's presence, I soon feel that Our Lord is calling me back to do what I ought to do. I do not know how to describe this voice that calls me. I know, though, that it is quite penetrating, and any soul that hears it can almost not refuse it.

Do not ask me, my father, how I know for sure that it is Our Lord who is showing himself to me in visions when I see nothing with my physical eyes or with the eyes of my spirit, because I do not know. I cannot say anything more than what I have said. I know only this: The one standing at my right side is Our Lord and no one else. And even before he told me who he was, my mind was already strongly impressed that it was he.

(To Fr. Benedetto of San Marco in Lamis, July 7, 1913)

July 9

If it happens that you suffer afflictions, whatever kind they may be, be assured that if you truly love God, everything will be turned to the good. Even when you cannot understand how any good could come of it, you can be very certain that it will undoubtedly come....

Do not lose heart about any failures, but stir up your confidence and deeper humility. Becoming discouraged or impatient after you slip is the result of a trick of the enemy. It means you are giving up your weapons, giving yourself up as conquered. You will not do this, though, because the Lord's grace is always at hand to help you.

(To Antonietta Vona, November 15, 1917)

July 10

What else can we desire except God's will? What else can souls conse-crated to him long for? What else can you desire except that his divine purposes are being accomplished in you? Be courageous, then, and always move forward on the paths of divine love, having the certitude that the more your will is united and conformed to God's will, the more it will increase in perfection!

Let us always be mindful that the earth is a battleground, but in para-dise we will receive a crown; the earth is the place of trial, but we will receive a prize above. We are in exile here on earth because heaven is our true home.

(To Raffaelina Cerase, June 24, 1915)

July 11

Let us turn out thoughts to heaven, our true home—earth is only its shadow.

May the reasons of faith and the comfort of Christian hope always sustain you in your suffering, and as you remember these, the bitterness of your trial will be sweetened by the heavenly Father with the balm of his goodness and mercy. In addition to the goodness and mercy of the heavenly Father,… faith counsels us and spurs us on to have recourse to insistent but humble prayer with the firm hope of being heard, confi-dent in the promise the divine Master gives us: "Ask, and it will be given you; seek, and you will find; knock, and it will opened to you" [Matthew 7:7], and, "If you ask anything of the Father, he will give it to you in my name" [John 16:23].

Yes, let us pray, let us always pray in the serenity of our faith and with tranquillity of soul.

(To Raffaelina Cerase, June 24, 1915)

July 12

I know you are saddened that you cannot effectively correct your imperfections. But take heart, my dearest sons, and remember what I have often told you about this: You need to be devoted equally to the practice of faithfulness to God and to the practice of humility. Faithfulness renews your resolution to serve God as often as you break it and helps you not to break it. Humility, when you fail to keep your resolution, helps you recognize your abject spiritual poverty.

Take great care to purify your hearts according to the number and magnitude of the inspirations you receive. Lift up your souls to God frequently; read good books as often as you can, but read them with great devotion. Be consistent in meditation, in prayer, and in an examination of conscience many times a day.

(To Franciscan novices, no date)

July 13

No matter how great the trial is that the Lord is making you undergo, no matter how unbearable your desolation of spirit is at certain times, never lose courage. Run to Jesus with childlike abandon, because he will not be able to resist letting you feel a bit of refreshment and comfort. Always run to him, even when the devil is showing you your sins to cast a pall over your days. Lift your voice up loudly to him with a humble spirit, a contrite heart, and a prayer on your lips.

It is impossible, Raffaelina, for God not to look kindly on these kinds of demonstrations and not give way and surrender. It is true that God's power triumphs over all, but humble, sorrowful prayer triumphs over God himself. It stops his arm, it turns away his wrath, it disarms him, it wins him over, it placates him and almost makes him deferential to you as a friend.

Oh! If all human beings knew this great secret of Christian life, taught to us by Jesus in word and deed and enacted by the publican in the temple and by Zacchaeus, Magdalene, St. Peter, and a host of other famous penitent and pious Christians, they would discover for themselves how much abundant fruit of holiness they could experience!

(To Raffaelina Cerase, September 7, 1915)

July 14

Do not distrust Divine Providence. Trust in God and abandon yourself to him; let him take care of you completely, and be calm so that you do not become confused. I understand and perceive how hard the trial is, how bitter the battle is. However, I also know that the fruit you will gather in time is very abundant. The crown being woven for you up above is far superior to any human concept of it.

…What I want from you is that as trials increase, your abandonment to God and trust in him may also increase. Always deepen your humility and your praises of the Lord, who deigns in his goodness to visit you to prepare you to be part of the construction of the heavenly Zion.

(To Raffaelina Cerase, April 10, 1915)

July 15

Nothing can terrify a soul who puts its trust in the Lord and places its hope in him. The enemy of our salvation is always lurking around trying to snatch from our hearts the anchor that leads us to salvation—by that I mean trust in God our Father. Let us hold this anchor very tightly and never allow it to be yielded up even for an instant. Otherwise all could be lost…. Always be vigilant not to think more highly of yourself because you consider yourself good at doing something. Do not lift yourself higher than others either, thinking that you are better than they are or at least their equal, but consider others better than yourself. The enemy, Raffaelina, conquers the proud but not the humble of heart.

(To Raffaelina Cerase, April 10, 1915)

July 16

I aspire to reach the light, but that light never comes. And if at times I see a few feeble rays of light, which rarely happens, it reawakens in my soul the most desperate longings to see the sun shining again. These longings are so strong and intense that very often they make me languish and pine with love for God so much that I am on the brink of swooning.

All of this happens without my looking for it or doing anything to make it happen. Most of the time it happens outside times of prayer and even when I am doing things of no importance.

I do not want to have these feelings, because I realize that when they are very intense, my body also has a strong reaction. I feel as if I am dying at every instant, and I would like to die so as not to feel the weight of God's hand bearing down on me.

What is all this? What do I need to do to get out of such a deplorable state? Is it God working in me, or is it something else? Speak to me clearly, as always, and help me understand how I should proceed.

(To Fr. Benedetto of San Marco in Lamis, July 16, 1917)

July 17

There are certain moments when I am assailed by intense temptations against faith. I am sure that my will is not involved, but my imagination is so stirred and the temptation lurking in my mind is so vivid that it presents sin not only as something casual but also as something worth desiring.

All of this is followed by thoughts of despondency, diffidence, desperation, and even—please do not be horrified, my father—blasphemy. I am frightened in the face of such a struggle. I tremble and I struggle violently, but I am certain that by God's grace I will not fall.

(To Fr. Benedetto of San Marco in Lamis, July 16, 1917)

July 18

The doubt that always assails me and follows me wherever I go is of not knowing if what I am doing is pleasing to God or not. I know that you have spoken to me about this many times, but what should I do during this harsh test if I forget everything you said? What if, even if I do have some recollection, I can recall nothing specific and everything gets all mixed up?

Oh! Could you please put it in writing one more time for me? God is now always growing larger in my mind's eye, but I always see him enveloped by a thick cloud in the heaven of my soul. I feel that he is near, but I can see him only from very far away. What increases my longing is that God becomes more intimate with me and I sense him, but these longings always make him seem even further away. My God! How strange this is!

(To Fr. Benedetto of San Marco in Lamis, July 16, 1917)

July 19

What is producing such desolation in your spirit is a very special grace
that God gives only to souls that he wants to draw into mystical union
with him. That is precisely what is happening, my dear Raffaelina.
Alarm and terror are the poor soul's reactions to this grace, if I am not
mistaken.

This grace is a very simple light, superlatively splendid and clear, that
affects the soul this way when it first comes. It finds the soul unprepared
and not well adapted to receive it, so it produces precisely the effect that
is happening in you at present. To prove this to you, or better, to give you
an analogy—although it does not directly apply to your situation—I ask
you to imagine someone who has an eye disease. This individual suffers
in seeing the light and could almost accuse the sun of being an enemy
to the eyes....

I conclude that the same thing is happening here for your soul because
it is now full of this kind of spiritual light. The soul finds itself somewhat sick and ill disposed to be able to receive this supernatural light.
The poor soul assailed by this light then experiences terror and fear in
its faculties, memory, intelligence, and will and indirectly experiences a
similar fear and terror even in the body. However, as the soul is being
healed of its indisposition little by little, it soon begins to feel the healing
effects of this new grace.

(To Raffaelina Cerase, February 28, 1915)

July 20

I would like our very gentle Jesus to bring peace to all afflicted hearts. I confess to you, most beloved daughter of Jesus, that my soul can sincerely say with the apostle Paul—although I do not have even an infinitesimal degree of the spirit of charity that burned in that holy apostle's heart— "I could wish that I myself were accursed and cut off from Christ for the sake of my brethren" [Romans 9:3]. Yes, I could wish that our most gentle Lord excommunicate me, separate me from himself, abandon me, leave me in disgrace with the punishments owed to my brethren, and remove me from the Book of Life—not in order to deprive me of his love and his grace, from which nothing can ever separate me, but in order to save my brothers and sisters, my companions in exile on earth. Pray to the Lord that he may satisfy these burning desires of mine.

(To Raffaelina Cerase, April 25, 1914)

July 21

You are grieved over the ingratitude of people toward God, and you do well to weep over their misdeeds. Offer God your praises and all your actions in reparation, making sure they are all good. However, after you have wept in secret for the misdeeds of others who are obstinate in their state of perdition, it is fitting that you imitate Our Lord and the apostles by taking your mind off that and turning it to other things and activities that are more useful to God's glory and the salvation of souls. In speaking to the Jews, the apostles said, "It was necessary that the word of God should be spoken first to you. Since you thrust it from you, and judge yourselves unworthy of eternal life, behold, we turn to the Gentiles" [Acts 13:46]. In the holy Gospel the divine Master says, "The kingdom of God will be taken away from you and given to a nation producing the fruits of it" [Matthew 21:43].

Grieving too long for people who are hardened in their sin would be a loss of valuable time that is needed for bringing salvation to our other brothers and sisters and working for the glory of God.

(To Raffaelina Cerase, April 25, 1914)

July 22

Jesus is making you, like all those who love him with sincere and pure hearts, increasingly hear his very loving threefold invitation: "Come to me.... Take my yoke upon you, and learn from me" [Matthew 11:28–29]. May this very sweet invitation from the Master comfort you in this new trial—or to be more precise, this increase in divine favor. I can truly say that your new state is a very special favor from the Lord, a favor that he accords only to those valiant souls that his mercy makes more precious to him.

Rejoice with me, then, for such significant kindness from our good God. Oh Raffaelina! How sweet and comforting it is for a soul to know that it is raised up by our very sweet Father to anointed dignity, although not through any merit of its own! Oh! Open your heart to this Father, the most loving of all fathers, and let him work in you freely. We should not be stingy with someone who enriches us so much and whose generosity has no end and knows no bounds or limits.

(To Raffaelina Cerase, March 4, 1915)

July 23

In all of life's events, recognize God's divine will, adore it, bless it. Do not be eager to free yourself from the things that are hard for you and particularly the things that are the hardest. Instead lift up your mind even more to the divine Father and tell him, "My life, like my death, is in your hands. Do with me what is most pleasing to you."

In times of spiritual oppression, say to him, "Lord, God of my heart, you alone know and understand completely the heart of every creature. You alone know my pain, you alone understand that all my anguish arises from my fear of losing you, of offending you, and of not loving you as much as you deserve and as much as I ought to and want to. If you, to whom everything is present and who alone can read the future, know that it is better for your glory and for my salvation that I be in this state, so be it. I do not ask to be delivered from it. Give me strength so that I can fight and obtain the prize of valiant souls."

(To Raffaelina Cerase, March 4, 1915)

July 24

I ask myself at times if there are some people who do not feel heavenly fire burning in their hearts, especially when they are before him in the Eucharist. That seems impossible to me, especially if that person is a priest or a religious....

What is it that I am feeling, my father? I have so much confidence in Jesus that even if I saw hell opened up before me and found myself on the threshold of the abyss, I would not worry, I would not despair, I would trust him.

This is the kind of trust that his gentleness inspires in me. When I begin to consider the great battles that have been won over the devil with heavenly assistance, they are too many to count.

Who knows how many times my faith would have vacillated and my hope and charity waned if he had not stretched out his hand to me? Who knows how many times my mind would have become darkened if Jesus, the Eternal One, had not illuminated it?

(To Fr. Agostino of San Marco in Lamis, December 3, 1912)

July 25

Let us humble ourselves deeply, my good father, and confess that if God were not our shield and armor, we would be constantly pierced by every kind of sin. For that reason we need to keep ourselves in God by persevering in our spiritual exercises, so let us be fervently attentive to perform them.

Let us always have the fires of charity burning in our hearts, and let us never lose heart. If some listlessness or weakness of spirit occurs in us, let us run to the foot of the cross. Let us surround ourselves with the fragrances of heaven, and we will undoubtedly be reinvigorated.

(To Fr. Agostino of San Marco in Lamis, July 24, 1917)

July 26

Let us be vigilant not to give the enemy any room to make inroads into our spirits and contaminate the temples of the Holy Spirit. Oh! For the sake of love, let us not ignore this great truth even for a moment. Let us always keep in mind that through baptism we became temples of the living God, and that each and every time we turn our souls to the world, the flesh, and the devil—the things we renounced in baptism—we profane the sacred temples of God.

Flee every shadow of imperfection that could make room for these three chief enemies to infiltrate your heart. Resist their assaults at all times with a lively faith nourished by abundant charity.

(To Raffaelina Cerase, May 13, 1915)

July 27

I know that our enemies are strong, very strong, but for the soul who fights them with Jesus, what doubt could there be about winning the victory? Oh! Isn't our God the strongest one of all? Who could resist him? Who can thwart his decrees and wishes? Hasn't he promised every soul that he will not allow it to be tempted beyond its strength? Is he not faithful to his promises? Is there anyone who believes that he is not? If there is such a person, do you want to know who it is? It is the foolish man, the madman: "The fool says in his heart, 'There is no God'" [Psalm 14:1] (when he is referring to the true God).

Oh Raffaelina! Whoever sins through unbelief, through a lack of trust, is also a madman. You have often had not one but an infinite number of proofs of this divine promise of victory.

(To Raffaelina Cerase, May 13, 1915)

July 28

If the grace of Jesus had not come to enlighten you and draw you to himself, you would be like the foolish man who is not aware that he has walked all night on the edge of a riverbank because of the darkness that surrounded him. When daybreak comes to warn him of the danger he is in, he disregards the light and continues on his path, defying the danger. Wretched man! At some point the ground gives way under his feet, and he falls in and drowns.

You too walked alongside a precipice for a good part of the night. However, the grace of Jesus was so powerful that it did not limit itself only to showing you and warning you of the danger you had been in until then; he also wanted to do more for you. He attracted you to himself with the power of love, without in the least going against your free will.

You experienced that loving power and could do nothing other than be conquered by it.

(To Raffaelina Cerase, November 4, 1914)

July 29

You are responding in the best way you can to the word "suffer" that Jesus spoke to you, so do not be depressed if it seems that you often go in search of Simon the Cyrene when your human nature is crying out for comfort. Because of that you feel that your love for God is not sincere or perfect, but that is not true. Even Jesus in his humanity, during the agony he freely accepted, prayed that the chalice be taken away. Can you conclude then…that the love of Jesus for his divine Father was less than perfect and sincere? I will let you answer that.

At times the spirit is willing but the flesh is weak. However, God is interested in our spirits more than anything else, so reach out to him more with your will, with that deepest part of your spirit. Let your natural self be resentful, get upset, and demand its rights, because nothing is more normal to the flesh than that.

(To Raffaelina Cerase, June 8, 1915)

July 30

What guilty person who is being punished does not object to his suffering, even if he realizes he deserves it, and does not demand to be free of it? Always keep in mind this general principle that when God tests us with crosses and suffering, he always leaves our spirits a glimmer of light by which we can maintain our great trust in him and see his immense goodness.

I exhort you, then, not to become completely dejected when facing a cross that heaven sends you, but keep alive an unlimited confidence in divine mercy. Oh Raffaelina, God loves you very much, and you are responding the best way you can to his love. He is not looking for anything else, so trust, hope, submit yourself to his divine workings, and love him.

(To Raffaelina Cerase, June 8, 1915)

July 31

Keep your resolutions: Stay in the boat in which the Lord has placed you, and let the storm come. Jesus is alive! You will not perish. He will be sleeping, but just at the right time he will wake up to restore the calm. Scripture tells us that our St. Peter became fearful when he saw the storm and cried out trembling, "Lord, save me." Our Lord, taking him by the hand, said to him, "O you of little faith, why did you doubt?" [Matthew 14:30, 31]. Observe this holy apostle, daughters. He was walking on the water with dry feet. The wind and the waves could not submerge him, but fear of the wind and waves made him lose heart. Fear is an evil worse than evil itself.

Oh daughters of little faith, what are you afraid of? No, do not fear. You are walking on the sea in the midst of the wind and the waves, but remember that you are with Jesus.

(To the Ventrella sisters, March 8, 1918)

AUGUST

August 1

Live a quiet life, my daughter. Follow the path on which God has placed you, and diligently try to satisfy and please Jesus, who suffered the abandonment of his Father out of love for us and whom the heavenly Father has willed for you to accompany. Like a bee, carefully make honey out of your holy devotions and beeswax out of your domestic duties. Your devotions will bring sweetness to the taste of Christ (who was nourished by honey when he lived in the world),…and your household duties will abound to his great glory because they serve to light the beeswax candle of edification for your neighbor. May God, who has taken you by the hand with special care, guide you to the harbor of our eternal salvation.

(To Annita Rodote, January 2, 1918)

August 2

There are moments when I feel as if I am dying. It is truly a miracle of divine mercy that I still continue to be alive. I am dying at every instant: I feel myself crucified by love....

Believe me, my Raffaelina, this very harsh time of mortification and trial, on top of the normal ones, is oppressive at times, and I feel as though I am crushed under its enormous weight. Sometimes I think it is divine chastisement for my countless acts of unfaithfulness to the goodness of the Divine Majesty, and for that reason all my prayers seem to be useless. Unfortunately, I deserve this punishment, but is it possible that my wickedness could ever be more powerful than the mercy of the heavenly Father? No, that could never be. Thank goodness for Jesus! He is with us, so we have nothing to fear.

(To Raffaelina Cerase, March 25, 1915)

August 3

Understand fully what a cloister signifies so that you make no mistake about it. It is the academy of sharp correction in which every soul must learn to have itself molded, planed, and polished, so that being well smoothed and leveled out, it can be united to God's will. The clear and obvious sign of perfection is the willingness to be corrected, since that is the chief fruit of humility, the virtue that makes us aware that we do indeed need correction.

The cloister is a hospital for the spiritually ill who want to be healed. To be healed they subject themselves to bloodletting, lances, razors, scalpels, probes, cauterization, and all the painful instruments and procedures of medicine.

(To Franciscan novices, January 18, 1918)

August 4

I was thinking a few days ago about what some people say about the halcyons, those small birds that make their nests on the shores of the sea. They make their nests rounded like balls, and they make them so tight that the water cannot penetrate them. There is a small opening at the very top to let in the air. This is where the halcyons keep their baby birds, so that they can roll around and float on the waves without having the nest fill up and be submerged. The air that comes in at the top functions as a counterweight, so that these little balls are never destroyed.

Oh my most beloved sons, how I long to have your hearts formed this way: sealed tight on all sides so that when the agitations and storms of the world, the flesh, and the devil come upon you unexpectedly, they will not be able to penetrate them. I would like your hearts to have no openings except at the very top part that opens to heaven so that you can breathe in and inhale Our Lord Jesus.

(To Franciscan novices, January 18, 1918)

August 5

My sons, for whom is such a nest made if not for the chicks of the halcyon who constructs it through the love of God and divine, heavenly affection? But while the halcyon is constructing its nest and its baby birds are still too young to withstand the tossing of the waves, God takes care of them in his compassion, preventing the sea from engulfing them.

Oh God! My dear sons, the supreme Goodness will also make the nests of your hearts secure with his holy love against the assaults of the enemy and keep them from being submerged.

Oh, how I love those birds that are surrounded by water but breathe only air, that hide themselves in the water but see only the sky. They float like fish but sing like birds. What I find captivating is that the anchor to keep them steady in the midst of the waves is above them and not below them.

Oh my good sons, may sweet Jesus be pleased to shape your hearts this way: Surrounded by the world and the flesh, you live in the spirit; in the midst of the vanities of this world, you live in heaven; living in the midst of human beings, you praise and love him with the angels. May the foundation of your hope always be on high and in paradise.

(To Franciscan novices, January 18, 1918)

August 6

Oh my soul's God, where are you? Where are you hiding yourself? Where can I find you? Where should I look for you? Don't you see, Jesus, that my soul wants to feel you at any cost? My soul seeks you everywhere, but I find you only in the fullness of your fury that floods my soul with intense agitation and bitterness....Who could ever explain the gravity of my situation? What I understand in the reflection of your light cannot be said in human language, and when I do try to express it in a stuttering fashion, I become conscious that what I said is not correct and is further away than ever from the truth of the facts.

My God! Am I to be deprived of you forever? I want to cry out and groan in an extremely loud voice, but I am very weak, and I do not have the strength to do it. Meanwhile I can do nothing except lift up this lament to your throne: My God, my God, why have you forsaken me?

(To Fr. Benedetto of San Marco in Lamis, October 17, 1918)

August 7

My soul is completely laid bare in that clear picture of my misery! My God! May I hold up under such a distressing sight. You have withdrawn your reflected light from me because I could not bear the vivid contrast it reveals. My father, I see all my wickedness and ingratitude in his light. I see the old ruined man of flesh, curled up into himself; he seems to want to pay God back for his absence by denying him the rights that are clearly due to him. What power is needed to deal with this old man! My God, come quickly to my assistance, because I fear for myself, a treacherous and ungrateful creature toward his Creator, who protects him from his powerful enemies.

I did not know how to avail myself of your lofty favors, so now I am condemned to living alone with my helplessness, turned in on myself in a state of derailment while your hand increasingly presses down on me. Alas! Who will deliver me from myself? Who will free me from this body of death? Who will extend a hand to me so that I do not become swallowed up by the vast, deep ocean? Do I need to resign myself to being caught up by the tempest that is always pursuing me more and more?…

Oh my father, please come to my assistance! My internal organs are flowing with blood, and at times my eyes are forced to see blood pour out of me as well. Oh! May this distress, this condemnation, this humiliation, this confusion cease! I am not able and do not know how to withstand this.

(To Fr. Benedetto of San Marco in Lamis, October 17, 1918)

August 8

I saw a tree in Rome that is said to have been planted by the patriarch St. Dominic. People come to see it and touch it fondly out of devotion and out of love for the one who planted it. Likewise, having seen the tree of desire for holiness that God himself has planted in your souls, I love it tenderly, and I feel pleasure in seeing it now more than before. Therefore I exhort you to have a similar reaction and to repeat with me: May God make you grow, Oh lovely tree planted by God. May God make you bring your fruit to maturity, and when you do, may it please God to preserve you from the harmful wind that makes ripe fruit fall to the ground, where wild animals come to devour it indiscriminately.

My dearest sons, this desire in you needs to be like the orange trees on the coast of Genoa, which, according to what people say, are simultaneously loaded with fruit, flowers, and leaves almost all year long. Your desires should always be bearing fruit on all the occasions that present themselves to you each day…. The tree's flowers are your intentions, and its leaves are the frequent acknowledgments of your weakness that preserve both your good works and your good desires.

(To Franciscan novices, January 18, 1918)

August 9

Yes, my soul is wounded with love for Jesus. I am sick with love; I continually experience the grievous pain of that fire that burns but does not consume. Tell me, if you can, what remedy there is for the current state of my soul.

Here is a pale comparison of what Jesus is doing in me: Just as a current in the depth of the ocean sweeps everything in its path along with it, so too my soul, deeply engulfed in that boundless ocean of Jesus' love—given not for any merit of my own and without my understanding it—sweeps along with it all of his treasures.

(To Fr. Agostino of San Marco in Lamis, August 9, 1912)

August 10

You will understand, my good daughter, why the soul that has chosen divine love cannot remain self-centered in the heart of Jesus but instead feels burning charity toward brothers and sisters, although they often make that soul suffer.

How does this all happen? Daughter, it is not difficult to understand, because the soul is no longer living its own life but the life of Jesus who is dwelling in it. The soul must feel, want, and live the same sentiments, wishes, and life of the one who lives in it. And you know, my very beloved daughter, even though you have learned it late, you do know, I tell you, what sentiments and wishes did and still do animate the heart of that divine Master toward God and humanity.

Let your soul long for God and for the people who do not want to know about him, because that attitude is highly pleasing to him.

(To one of the Campanile sisters, May 31, 1918)

August 11

The dark picture of my past is added [to these temptations] in which I see only my wretchedness and ingratitude toward God. My heart is wracked with pain, and extreme confusion comes over me. I feel as though I were being excessively tortured and all my bones were being crushed and dislocated.

And I feel this harsh process not only in the hidden recesses of my spirit but also in my body as well. Then a strong fear attacks me that perhaps God is not the author of this strange phenomenon because, if he were, how could this physical upheaval be explained?

(To Fr. Benedetto of San Marco in Lamis, July 16, 1917)

August 12

Recalling the wonders of that time [of St. Francis and St. Clare], I think of the beloved first female disciple of the seraphic father in the deep and solemn silence of the austere refectory....

One day there was only one loaf of bread left in the convent, and it was lunchtime. Although the sisters had overcome their hunger pains, they could not ignore the imperious necessities of life forever. Sr. Cecilia, in the refectory, explained the situation to the holy abbess, who ordered the loaf be cut in two: one half for the brothers who were keeping watch in the monastery and one half for the sisters. She instructed that the half loaf for the sisters be divided into fifty portions, the number of sisters.... But when the devoted daughter responded that the ancient miracles of Jesus would be needed in order to divide the small half loaf into fifty parts, St. Clare responded, "Proceed exactly the way I instructed you."

The obedient daughter hurried to fulfill her command, and Mother Clare hurried to Jesus in prayer with pitiful sighs for her daughters. By divine grace the half loaf multiplied in the hands of the one who broke it, and each sister had a copious portion.

(To Graziella Pannullo, December 30, 1921)

August 13

On another day the handmaid of the Lord [Clare] had just arrived and could not prepare the food for the sisters who were ill because there was no oil. St. Clare, the mistress of humility, took the container, washed it herself, put it in the special place in the wall, and sent for a brother to go beg for some oil. Br. Bentivegna hurried to come to the aid of the poor sisters. However, before he arrived, the oil jar had been filled with oil through divine mercy, since St. Clare's prayer of faith anticipated the accommodation of the Father to relieve her poor daughters. The poor brother, thinking that he had been called in vain, murmured, "Perhaps these sisters called on me to play a joke on me because the jar is full." He looked around to see who might have brought the oil, but there was no one there. The Lord had come miraculously to help those who had abandoned everything for him, and he bowed obediently to the desire of his spouse who had called on him with the purity and faith that can move mountains.

(To Graziella Pannullo, December 30, 1921)

August 14

Do not be afraid if you feel nothing during your meditation, prayer, and other devout practices, or if you feel yourself still tied to earthly things, or if you still experience the conflict between the old man and the new man, or if you see yourself still beset by weakness. Since you are not choosing any of this, you are not culpable. In fact, all of that is a source of merit for you.

These are the trials of a soul that God loves. He wants to test that soul when he sees it has enough strength to withstand the battle and to weave a wreath of glory with its own hands.

(To one of the Campanile sisters, January 1919)

August 15

Oh God! Let my poor heart always experience you, and fulfill the work that you have begun in me.

I hear an inner voice that tells me passionately, "Sanctify yourself and sanctify others." Well then, my dearest one, I want to do that, but I do not know where to begin.

Help me. I know that Jesus loves you very much, and you have won his love. Therefore speak to him for me, that he may give me the grace to be a son who is more worthy of St. Francis and that I may be an example to my fellow friars in such a way that my fervor continues and increases more and more at all times to make me a perfect Capuchin.

(To one of the Campanile sisters, November 1922)

August 16

What can I tell you about myself? I am a mystery to myself....

My father, when will the sun shine again in the heaven of my soul? Alas! I find myself confounded in the deep and profound night I am experiencing. But God is alive—he who does not abandon any of those who hope in him and trust in him!

What is there to tell you about my physical state? I would prefer not to talk about that, since that issue is of no importance to me. I only long for God to come and strike his last blow.

(To Fr. Agostino of San Marco in Lamis, August 15, 1916)

August 17

The sorrow of love is sweet, and its burden is light. Why therefore do you go around saying, when you experience a great transport, that you do not know how to bear it? Your heart is small, but it is able to expand, and when it can no longer contain the immensity of the Beloved and is resistant to his enormous pressure, do not fear, because he is within you and outside you. Pouring himself into you, he will strengthen the walls of your heart. Like a seashell at the ocean, you will drink to your satisfaction, and you will be surrounded by exuberance and carried by its power.

In a very short while, you will not be a novice in these new characteristics of Love, and his assaults will no longer be overwhelming for you. Growing accustomed to the familiar flames, you will be able to summon him to a contest, and you will struggle as Jacob did with the angel without being thrown down to the ground.

(To Girolama Longo, July 29, 1920)

August 18

Blessed be God, who alone knows how to work wonders in a soul that is always recalcitrant toward him, a receptacle of infinite impurities. He chose to make me an example of his grace. He wants to use me as an example for all sinners, so that no one gives up hope. May sinners fix their gaze on me, the greatest of sinners, and put their hope in God.

Sinners, focus your attention on me, a most unholy person, and be encouraged not to despair of your salvation. Not only has the Lord forgiven me my sins, but he has also chosen to enrich me with his most precious graces....

Forgive me. It is a fool who is madly in love with his God who is speaking to you, so he deserves your forbearance.

(To Raffaelina Cerase, November 16, 1914)

August 19

May God's kingdom come quickly. May our very merciful Father sanctify his church. May he pour out his mercy abundantly on the souls who have not yet come to know him. May Satan's kingdom be destroyed, and may all his wicked schemes be exposed, to the consternation of that hellish beast. May all the souls enslaved by this sorry so-and-so know what a liar he is. May our most tender Father enlighten the minds of all human beings and touch their hearts, so that the fervent do not grow cold and slacken on their road to salvation, so that the lukewarm become zealous, and so that those who are far off return to him. May he scatter and confound all the learned of this world so that they do not war against and impede the spread of his kingdom. Finally, may the thrice-holy Father remove far from his church every existing division and prevent others from arising, so that there will be only one flock and one Shepherd. May the Lord multiply the number of elect souls a hundredfold. May he send forth many holy and learned ministers and sanctify those that have already been sent out. Through them may he restore fervor to all Christian souls.

(To Annita Rodote, March 8, 1915)

August 20

God commands us to love him but not as much and how he deserves, because he knows our capabilities, and so he does not command or require from us what we cannot do. Instead he commands us to love him according to our strength with all our soul, all our mind, and all our heart. Well then, aren't you trying to do that? And if you do not succeed, why groan about it? Why become agitated? God knows full well our intention, which is righteous and holy in his eyes. God knows full well why he allows so many good desires not to be carried out unless great effort is expended, and why some never do succeed at all. Even when this happens, there is no reason to be distressed uselessly, since there is always some gain or profit for the soul from such failures. If a person gains nothing more than mortification from it, that would be a great thing!

(Unknown addressee, June 3, 1917)

August 21

Open your heart to the heavenly physician of souls and abandon yourself confidently into his most holy arms. He is dealing with you as someone chosen to follow Jesus up the steep slope of Calvary, and I rejoice to see that grace working in you. Rest assured that everything taking place in your soul is ordained by the Lord, so do not be afraid of encountering any harm, as that fear would be offensive to God.

Be at peace that you are not offending the Lord in any way; on the contrary, he is being glorified through all this.

(To Raffaelina Cerase, May 19, 1914)

August 22

Live in a humble, gentle way, in love with our heavenly Bridegroom. Do not be troubled about not remembering all your minor shortcomings for confession. No, daughter, it is not right for you to grieve about this, because you often fall without realizing it, and similarly you get back up again without realizing it.

…With honesty and humility about the failures you can recall, refer them to the gentle mercy of God, who places his hand beneath those who fall without choosing to lest they harm or wound themselves. He also lifts them up and comforts them so quickly that they are unaware they have fallen because his divine hand caught them as they fell. They are unaware they have been lifted up because this happens so quickly that they have no time to notice it.

(To one of the Campanile sisters, October 18, 1917)

August 23

Last Friday I was in church giving thanks for the Mass when all at once my heart was wounded by a fiery arrow that burned so fiercely I thought I would die.

I do not have adequate words to describe the intensity of this flame; in fact, I am incapable of expressing it. Believe me! When the soul is a victim of these consolations, it becomes mute. It seemed to me an invisible force was completely immersing me into fire…. My God! What fire! What sweetness!

I have not experienced many transports of love like this, and at various times it is as though I were out of this world. At other times, however, this fire has been less intense. This time, instead, if it had lasted one more instant, one more second, my soul would have separated from my body, and I would have gone away with Jesus.

What a wonderful thing it is to become a victim of love!

(To Fr. Agostino of San Marco in Lamis, August 26, 1912)

August 24

You have every reason to be terrified if you try to measure the level of battle against your strength, but knowing that Jesus does not leave you for one instant should be the best consolation. God himself tells us that he is with the afflicted and those in tribulation: "I will be with him in trouble" [Psalm 91:15]. He comes down to wipe away the tears from their eyes. Be comforted, then, with the sweet thought that after such dense darkness, the lovely afternoon sun will shine. You will contemplate our heavenly Bridegroom in that light with a very pure and simple gaze. Do not allow yourself to believe, my most beloved sister, that you are practically a derelict in the Lord's eyes and there is no salvation for you. Reject that idea, which comes from our common enemy.

(To Raffaelina Cerase, January 23, 1915)

August 25

Pray fervently, and you will then have victory over your enemies. Humble yourself under the mighty hand of the heavenly Physician, and when the wedding feast is celebrated, Jesus will have you sit in the highest place, since God promises that those who humble themselves will be exalted.

Always offer fervent thanksgiving to God through Jesus Christ, and you will thus dispose yourself very well to receive other favors from heaven. In contrast, the one who does not bother to appreciate the favors already received is quite naturally unworthy of future favors.

(To Raffaelina Cerase, September 28, 1915)

August 26

Your imagination and the devil want you to believe that you are continually offending God and that you are always, or almost always, resisting divine calls. The vigilant grace of the heavenly Father keeps you at a safe distance from falling into such infidelities. Be reassured on this point. I assure you that thoughts like those are coming only from your imagination and the devil. Guard yourself from giving them any importance. They have no other aim than to cool your feelings of affection toward the heavenly Bridegroom and to trouble you about attaining Christian perfection by pointing out how difficult and impossible it is for you. And what is worse, these thoughts aim more directly to dry up or drain off whatever feelings of devotion are in your heart.

(To Raffaelina Cerase, August 15, 1914)

August 27

During a period of dryness of spirit, be humble, patient, and yielded to the divine will, and do not neglect doing the things you used to do in times of spiritual joy. Genuine love does not consist in having many consolations when you are serving God but in having a willingness to be ready to do everything that God is pleased to ordain for your spiritual advantage and for his glory.

Believe this, and it does not matter if you have to force yourself to believe it and are not able to understand the reason for the dryness. The martyrs also believed this when they were suffering. The most beautiful *credo,* "I believe," is the one we say during times of sacrifice and through a stringent exercise of our wills.

(To Erminia Gargani, December 6, 1916)

August 28

The fear you say you have about sins committed in the past is decep-
tive and is a genuine torment caused by the devil. Haven't you already
confessed those sins? Well, what are you afraid of? Let that whole sad
affair go once and for all, and instead open your heart wide to a holy
and boundless confidence in Jesus. Trust that he is not the cruel bill col-
lector that the devil makes him out to be. Rather he is the Lamb who
takes away the sins of the world, interceding with unspeakable groans
for our salvation.

(To Raffaelina Cerase, March 29, 1914)

August 29

It is not true that you have been driven away by Jesus, as you believe.
Oh! Trust in him fearlessly, because you have every reason to do so. It is
not abandonment but love itself that our very sweet Savior is demonstrating to you. I do not have words enough to thank the goodness of
the Lord, who treats you so lovingly and protects you. Do not believe
the evil one when he tries to convince you that you are being victim-
ized by his assaults and by divine abandonment. He wants to deceive
you. Spurn him in the name of Jesus and his most holy mother.

(To Raffaelina Cerase, March 29, 1914)

August 30

By God's will I continue to be in poor health. But what causes the worst suffering are those strong sharp pains in my chest. At certain times I feel such great agony that it seems the pain is breaking my back and my chest. However, Jesus never stops soothing my sufferings from time to time in another way, by speaking to me in my heart. Oh yes, my father! How good Jesus is to me! Oh, what precious moments those are! That happiness has no comparison. It is a happiness that the Lord lets me taste almost only in times of affliction.

At those times, more than ever, everything that is of the world is repugnant to me, and I have no other desire than to love and suffer. Yes, my father, even in the midst of so much suffering I am happy, because I seem to feel my heart beating along with Jesus' heart.

(To Fr. Benedetto of San Marco in Lamis, September 4, 1910)

August 31

It is true that the temptations that I am being subjected to are very considerable, but I trust in Divine Providence to keep me from falling into the snares of the insidious one. It is also true that Jesus very often hides himself, but what does that matter? With his assistance I will seek to be around him at all times, since you have assured me that these things do not indicate an abandonment but are games of love.

Oh! How I long in these moments to have someone to help me temper the anxieties and the flames that are agitating my heart right now!

(To Fr. Benedetto of San Marco in Lamis, September 4, 1910)

September 1

Reject what the enemy is powerfully suggesting to your soul in wanting you to believe that you are on the verge of being lost. Scorn such malignant insinuations and live at peace, because the Lord is with you in your tribulations now more than ever. Sacred Scripture also assures us that an afflicted soul is united to God: "I am with him in trouble," says God [Psalm 91:15]. Take heart, then, and do not fear, because it is certain that the soul that fears being lost is not lost; it is certain that the soul that fights while fixing its gaze on God will sing a victory song and intone a hymn of triumph. There is nothing for you to fear, my Raffaelina, since we are promised the necessary help by the heavenly Father not to be overcome by temptation.

(To Raffaelina Cerase, April 10, 1915)

September 2

When the enemy wants to insinuate himself into your heart to conquer it with a fear about the past, consider the past to be swallowed up in the sea of heavenly goodness. Concentrate on the present, in which Jesus is with you and loves you. Think about the future, when Jesus will reward your faithfulness and surrender, or—even better—think about all the graces that he has lavished on you and still bestows on you continually that you have certainly never deliberately misused. Therefore, insofar as it is possible—because no one is expected to do the impossible—you should pray to put aside every fear and to have confidence, faith, and love at all times.

Sr. Thérèse of the Child Jesus used to say that we would be judged by our love!

(To Raffaelina Cerase, October 8, 1915)

September 3

Jesus wants to toss you, shake you, pound you, and sift you like wheat so that your spirit attains the level of cleanliness and purity that he desires. Should wheat ever be put in the barn if the weeds and chaff have not been removed? Should linen ever be kept in the house if it has not first been made white? This is also what should happen to an elect soul.

I understand that temptations seem to stain rather than purify the soul, but that is hardly the case. Let us hear what the saints have to say about this matter. It should be enough for you to know that the great St. Francis de Sales says temptations are like soap: When his clothes are full of soapy water, they seem to be dirty, but in fact the soap makes them clean.

(To Raffaelina Cerase, April 11, 1914)

September 4

Do not agonize over the countless temptations that are continually assaulting you, because the Holy Spirit forewarns the devout soul that is disposed to advance in the ways of God to get ready, to prepare for temptation. For that reason take heart; the certain infallible sign of a soul's election to salvation is temptation. The poor soul in the midst of such a storm will be given that sign of contradiction. May reflection on the lives of all the saints who were not exempt from this trial help you bear up under your own trial.

Temptation spares no elect soul. It did not spare even the Apostle to the Gentiles, who, after having been taken up into paradise while he was still alive, underwent such a trial that Satan almost succeeded in overcoming him. My God! Who can read his writing without feeling the blood run cold in their veins! How many tears, how many sighs, how many groans, how many prayers did this holy apostle lift up to the Lord, asking him to remove this very painful trial from him! But how did Jesus answer? He answered nothing other than "My grace is sufficient for you," and "My power is made perfect in weakness" [2 Corinthians 12:9].

(To Maria Gargani, September 4, 1916)

September 5

If you are scorned by the world, rejoice because its hatred is primarily directed to the Author of life, the divine Master. If you are dismayed and afflicted with all kinds of deprivations, temptations, and trials from the devil and his followers, lift up your gaze and increase your courage. The Lord is with you, so there is no room for fear.

The enemy will wage war against you, but he will never be able to bite you. Fight back hard. Always fight against the appetites of the flesh, worldly vanity, and the seduction of gold and high social standing— the things the enemy is always using against us. The conflict is hard, of course, and the battle is painfully won, but *sursum corda!*—"Let us lift up our hearts" [Lamentations 3:41]—and keep your gaze fixed on high.

(To Maria Gargani, September 4, 1916)

September 6

My present state leaves much to be desired, my father. I feel a great protraction of my strength. I see crosses added on to crosses, sorrows added on to sorrows, and I will not be able to withstand them if the immediate intervention of the heavenly Father does not sustain me with his omnipotent arm.

Bitter spiritual battles are added to my physical difficulties. Very dark clouds are always gathering in the sky of my poor soul. It is true that Jesus is always with me, but how painful, my father, is the trial that risks making my soul offend the divine Bridegroom! But God is forever alive! My confidence to overcome and emerge victorious and the strength to continue the fight are not decreasing.

(To Fr. Agostino of San Marco in Lamis, September 7, 1914)

September 7

May infinite thanks be given to the merciful Jesus for having wiped away the tears of the church [at the death of Pope Pius X] and for having consoled her widowhood by sending her a new leader, so that everything would go according to God's wishes. Let us offer our good wishes to the new pontiff, that he will be a worthy successor of the great Pope Pius X, a truly noble and holy soul that Rome has never seen the likes of before.

Born of the populace, he never forgot his humble beginnings. He was truly a supremely good shepherd, a very peaceful ruler, and a gentle and meek Jesus on earth. Oh! We will remember the good pope and fervently lift up prayers for the repose of this great soul, but we will remember him even more now as an intercessor close to the Most High.

(To Fr. Agostino of San Marco in Lamis, September 7, 1914)

September 8

Last night something happened to me that I can neither explain nor understand. In the middle of the palms of my hands, some redness appeared almost in the shape of a small coin, accompanied by a strong, sharp pain in the middle of that redness. The pain was more intense in my left hand, so much so that I can still feel it. I also feel a bit of pain under my feet.

This phenomenon has been going on for about a year, but it has been some time now since it has happened. Do not be upset that this is the first time I am mentioning it to you, because I am always blocked by my infernal self-consciousness. If you only knew how much I had to force myself even now to tell you about it! I have many things to say, but the words escape me. I will only say that when I am with Jesus in the Blessed Sacrament, the beating of my heart is so strong that it sometimes seems my heart is bursting out of my chest.

At the altar at times I feel such a burning throughout my whole being that I cannot describe it. It seems to me that my face is completely on fire. I do not understand, my father, what these signs mean.

(To Fr. Benedetto of San Marco in Lamis, September 8, 1911)

September 9

Live wholly in God, and for the sake of the love that bears you up, be patient with yourself in all your troubles. Remember that being good servants of God does not mean constant comfort, continual sweetness, and freedom from all aversions or recoiling from the good. If that were the case, neither St. Catherine of Siena, nor St. Teresa, nor St. Paul would have served the Lord well.

What matters in being good servants of God is being charitable to our neighbor, having an inviolable resolution at the core of our being to do God's will, having deep humility and simplicity in entrusting ourselves to God, and getting back up every time we fall. It means putting up with ourselves in our abjection and failures and quietly forbearing the imperfections of others.

(Unknown addressee, August 4, 1917)

September 10

In spiritual conflicts you need to do what the violin player does. When he hears something out of tune, he does not snap the string or walk away from the violin. Instead he immediately bends down to discover the source of discord, and then he patiently and gently stretches or relaxes the string as needed.

Well, do the same thing. Do not become impatient with troublesome things. Do not try to snap the string as soon as you hear a note out of tune, but be patient. Humble yourself before God. Gently stretch out or relax the strings of your heart before the heavenly Musician, because he can fix the disharmony.

(To Maria Gargani, November 22, 1916)

September 11

When you are attending Mass and other religious services, be very reverent when you stand up, kneel, and sit. Perform each action with great devotion. Be modest in your gaze, and do not turn your head this way and that to see who is coming or going. Out of reverence for that holy place, do not laugh or look around to see who is nearby. Try not to talk to anyone unless charity or a strict need requires it.

If you are reciting a group prayer, pronounce the words of the prayer distinctly, stop for the pauses, and never hurry through the prayer.

In short, behave in such a way that all the bystanders are edified and, because of you, are moved to glorify and love the heavenly Father.

When you leave the church, have a calm and collected demeanor.

(To Annita Rodote, July 25, 1915)

September 12

Your Holiness,

…The Capuchin Order has always been foremost in love, faithfulness, obedience, and devotion to the Apostolic See. I pray to the Lord that this will continue to be the case and that our order will continue in its tradition of religious conscientiousness and austerity, evangelical poverty, faithful observance of its rules and constitutions, renewing itself in its inner vitality of spirit according to the directives of Vatican Council II so as to be ready at all times to respond quickly to the needs of mother church, when Your Holiness calls on us.

I know that your heart is suffering deeply these days about the future of the church, about peace in the world, about people's needs, but especially about the failure even by some Catholics to obey the profound teaching that you, assisted by the Holy Spirit and in the name of God, give us. I offer you my daily prayers and sufferings, a small but sincere offering from the least of your sons, so that the Lord may comfort you with his grace to continue on the straight but difficult path of defending eternal truth, which never changes with the passing of time.

(To Pope Paul VI, September 12, 1968)

September 13

In addition, in the name of my spiritual children and the prayer groups, I thank you for your clear, definitive words, especially in your latest encyclical, *Humanae Vitae*, and I reaffirm my faith and unconditional obedience to your enlightened directives.

May the Lord cause truth to triumph. May he give peace to his church and tranquility to the nations of the earth. May he give health and prosperity to Your Holiness, so that these passing clouds are dispersed and the reign of God's kingdom comes to all hearts through your apostolic work as the Supreme Shepherd of all Christianity.

(To Pope Paul VI, September 12, 1968)

September 14

Pray to the divine Lover, this beloved Bridegroom of our souls, that he will complete the work of grace that he has begun in my humble soul. He has demonstrated in me, his poor abject creature, signs of very special favor since birth. He showed me that he would not only be my Savior and my greatest benefactor but also my devoted, sincere, and faithful friend, my heart's companion, my eternal and infinite love, my consolation, my joy, my comfort, my whole treasure.

But my heart, always fervent in love both for the All and for *everything*, is poured out, alas! even innocently and unconsciously on created things that are charming and pleasing to me. He is always watching over me, so he recaptured my heart and gently reproved me in a fatherly manner, yes, but the reproof is what my soul felt.

(To Maria Campanile, November 1922)

September 15

A melancholic but very sweet voice was echoing in my heart. It was the warning of a loving father who was outlining for his son the dangers that he would encounter in the warfare of life. It was the voice of a benevolent father who wanted to detach the heart of his son from childish, innocent loves. It was the voice of a loving father whispering into the ear and heart of his son to turn away from all the world's clay and dirt, jealously wanting him to consecrate himself entirely to him.

Passionately, with loving sighs and ineffable groans, with soft, sweet words, he called the son to himself and wanted to make him wholly his own....

And I, the ungrateful son, then understood it all and clearly contemplated the terrible and frightful picture that his infinite mercy was presenting to me [if I did not give myself to him], a truly disillusioning picture that would have made even the most tested souls tremble and fear.

...I understood that the safe harbor, the refuge of peace, for me was to belong to the ranks of the church militant.

(To Maria Campanile, November 1922)

September 16

Where could I serve you better, Lord, if not in the cloister and under the banner of the Poverello of Assisi [St. Francis]? And he [the Lord], seeing my bewilderment, smiled at me, and he smiled at me for a long time. That smile left an unspeakable sweetness in my heart. At times I truly felt him close by, and it seemed to me I saw his shadow, and my flesh, my whole being, exulted in God, my Savior.

And then I felt the two forces inside me that were quarrelling and tearing my heart apart: the world that wanted me for itself and the God who was calling me to a new life. My God! Who could ever recount the martyrdom that was happening inside me?

Merely recalling the internal battle that was going on makes my blood run cold, even though almost twenty years have passed.

I heard the voice of duty that I should obey you, the true and good God! But your enemies and mine terrorized me; they dislocated my bones, they mocked me, and they twisted my inner organs.

I wanted to obey you, Oh my God, my Bridegroom. That was the preeminent intention of my mind and desire of my heart.

(To Maria Campanile, November 1922)

September 17

You know, Lord, the hot tears I shed before you in those extraordinarily distressing times of that battle! You know, God of my soul, the groans of my heart, the tears that streamed from my eyes. You had the unmistakable sign of those tears and of what I was going through from the pillows that remained soaking wet. I wanted, and have always wanted, to obey you, but life in this world was blocking me. I wanted to die rather than shrink back from your call.

But you, Lord, who made this son of yours experience all the effects of a genuine abandonment, finally rose up, extended your mighty hand to me, and led me to the place where you had first called me. May infinite praise and thanks be given to you, my God.

You hid me here from the eyes of everyone. You had entrusted this son of yours with a very great mission since that time, a mission that only you and I know about. My God! My Father! How did I respond to such a mission?

I am not sure. I only know that I should have done more, and that is the reason for the current disquiet in my heart.

I sense that disquiet increasing during these days of spiritual retreat.

(To Maria Campanile, November 1922)

September 18

Oh Lord, rise up one more time, and free me henceforth from all of myself, and do not allow this son to be lost, the one you have attentively and kindly called and pulled back from the world that is not yourself. Rise up, therefore, one more time, Lord, and establish by your grace those whom you have entrusted to me, and do not allow any of them to be lost by their deserting the fold.

… Do not let your inheritance be lost. Oh God! Always be attentive to the cry of my humble heart, and complete the work you have begun in me.

(To Maria Campanile, November 1922)

September 19

It seems to me that the more a soul has been enriched, the more reason it has to humble itself before the Lord. As the gifts from the Lord increase, the soul can never fully repay the giver of every good. So then, what in particular do you have to boast about? What do you have that you did not receive? And if you have received everything, what do you boast about as though it were something that belonged to you?

Oh, repeat to yourself whenever the tempter wants you to swell with pride, "All the good that is in me I received from God as a loan. I would be a fool to boast about what is not mine." Deal with it that way, and do not be afraid.

(To Raffaelina Cerase, January 30, 1915)

September 20

On the morning of the twentieth last month [September], in the chancel after the celebration of holy Mass, I was surprised by a state of repose that was similar to a sweet sleep. All my inner and external senses as well as the faculties of my soul were suspended in an indescribable stillness. There was complete silence around and inside of me. Suddenly a great peace and a surrender to the complete loss of everything entered into me.... It all happened in an instant.

While this was happening, I found myself before a mysterious person like the one I saw on the evening of August 5 who was different only in this way: His hands, feet, and side were dripping with blood.

The sight terrified me. I do not know how to describe what I felt at that instant. I felt as if I were dying, and I would have died if the Lord had not intervened to strengthen my heart, which I felt was about to burst out of my chest.

My vision of this person was withdrawn, and I became aware that my hands, feet, and side were pierced and dripping with blood. Imagine the torment I felt then and that I am constantly experiencing almost every day.

(To Fr. Benedetto of San Marco in Lamis, October 22, 1918)

September 21

The wound in my heart spurts out blood regularly, especially from Thursday night to Saturday. My father, I am moving around in pain from the torture and for the subsequent confusion that I feel in the depth of my soul. I am afraid of dying from loss of blood if the Lord does not hear the groans of my poor heart and does not rescue me out of this predicament. Will Jesus, who is so good, grant me this grace?

Will he at least take away my confusion about these external signs? I will lift up my voice to him loudly, and I will not desist in begging that by his mercy he would take away not the torment or the pain from me…but these external signs, which cause me an indescribable and unbearable confusion and embarrassment.

(To Fr. Benedetto of San Marco in Lamis, October 22, 1918).

September 22

Jesus likes to communicate with simple souls. Let us try to acquire this good virtue, and let us hold it in great esteem. Jesus said, "Unless you turn and become like children, you will never enter the kingdom of heaven" [Matthew 18:3]. Before teaching us this through his words, however, he practiced it by his actions. He made himself a baby and gave us an example of the simplicity that he later taught through his words. Let us keep our hearts on the alert to stay far away from all worldly wisdom. Let us strive at all times to have pure thoughts, righteous ideas, and holy intentions in our minds.

Let us always keep our wills seeking nothing but God and his glory. If we attempt to advance in this lovely virtue, the one who taught it to us will always enrich us with new insights and greater heavenly favors.

Let us always keep before the eyes of our minds our status as priests, until we can join St. Paul in sincerely saying to every kind of person, "Be imitators of me, as I am of Christ" [1 Corinthians 11:1]. Let us not stop moving forward in this lovely virtue of simplicity.

However, we will not move one step forward in this virtue if we do not make every effort to live in holy and immutable peace.

(To Fr. Agostino of San Marco in Lamis, July 10, 1915)

September 23

Peace is simplicity of spirit, serenity of mind, quietness of soul, and the bond of love. Peace is the order, the harmony within us. It is the continuous contentment that comes from the testimony of a clear conscience. It is the holy joy of a heart in which God reigns. Peace is the road to perfection—or rather, perfection is found in peace. The devil, who knows all of this quite well, applies all his efforts to make us lose our peace.

Let us be on high alert against the least sign of turmoil, and as soon as we notice we have fallen into discouragement, let us have recourse to God with filial confidence and complete abandonment of ourselves to him.

Every instance of turmoil in us is very displeasing to Jesus, because it is always connected to some imperfection in us that has its origin in egotism or self-love.

(To Fr. Agostino of San Marco in Lamis, July 10, 1915)

September 24

There is only one thing the soul should regret, and that is offending God. We need to be very careful on this point. We should remember our failings, yes, but with peaceful sorrow, trusting in divine mercy at all times.

In addition, let us guard ourselves from certain reproofs to ourselves and self-condemnation, because those reproofs most often come from the enemy so that he can disturb our peace in God.

If any reproofs or regrets humble us and make us diligent in doing good without removing our trust in God, then we can be sure they come from God. However, if they muddle us and make us fearful, mistrustful, lazy, or slow to do good, then we can be sure they come from the devil, and, because they are such, we should chase them away and take refuge in our trust in God.

(To Fr. Agostino of San Marco in Lamis, July 10, 1915)

September 25

The shadows that surround your spirit are none other than the effects of the withdrawal of reflected light from your soul. The Lord, however, has replaced that reflected light with another light that is much brighter and more intense. This light is no different from the very light that will join the creature to the Creator in heavenly marriage one day.

You should not wonder if this profound light produces diverse effects and, I would say, almost contradictory effects, because it does not depend on the various dispositions or states of a soul when it is operating. First of all, this light causes the soul distress because it uncovers stains that the soul has never seen before, and what it sees would usually be seen only up above.

There are many other reasons for the soul to find itself distressed by this light, but there is one more than any other that torments this beloved of God. As soon as the soul has been penetrated by this very profound light, it does not yet see God as a loving Father but as a very severe judge. And far from blaming God for that, the soul, full of terror, accuses itself as the one and only cause of so much unhappiness.

(To Margherita Tresca, March 1916)

September 26

The soul that is so passionate for God does not see itself at all for what it is. It thinks it does not love him in the least, and no matter how the poor soul tries to love him, it seems that the Lord is not accepting that love and is even pushing it away.

This is the source of the soul's absolute conviction that it is forever rejected by God with no hope for his return. However, despite that conviction, the soul does not despair. Its outcry to heaven becomes more passionate. It continually knocks at the door of the divine host, even though it is persuaded the door will never be opened and that heaven will never stretch forth its scepter in the soul's direction.

Poor dear! How does one bear up under this? Who is there really to hold this soul up? The soul ought to realize that God, whom the soul considers far away, is actually within it and is working a process in it whose activity and efficacy are on a par with his love for his creatures.

That, in short, is an exposition of the current state of your soul. Your part is to submit yourself to it, to bless the hand that is leading you on a rare path indeed, but a very sure path for fruit that will accrue to your spirit.

(To Margherita Tresca, March [no date], 1916)

September 27

How many courtiers are there who come and go a hundred times in the presence of the king not to speak with or listen to him but solely to be seen by him and make themselves known as his genuine servants through their diligence? This approach to being in God's presence—to declare mainly by our will that we consider ourselves his servants—is very holy, excellent, and pure; it represents the greatest perfection. He will speak to you, he will indeed take a hundred walks in your company on the avenues in his garden of prayer. But when that does not happen anymore,…then be content because our duty is to be with him, considering what a great honor and grace it is for us that he allows us to be in his presence.

In this latter situation you should not feel uneasy about talking to him, because this other way of staying close to him is not less profitable but is actually much more profitable even though it is less to our liking. When, therefore, you find yourself close to God in prayer, depending on your current situation, either talk to him if you can or, if you cannot, at least stay put and make yourself be seen.

(To the Campanile sisters, August 23, 1918)

September 28

The greater your suffering, so much greater is God's love for you. May these trials be for you a marker of God's love for you. You will recognize God's love for you by this sign: the afflictions he sends you…. Exult, therefore, in the very raging of the tempest. Exult, I tell you, with the sons and daughters of God, because this love is the very unique love of the divine Bridegroom for you. Humble yourself again before his divine majesty, and think about how many other people there are in the world who are worthier and more endowed with intellectual gifts and virtues than you are, yet they are not treated with this unique love with which God has been treating you.

(To Raffaelina Cerase, September 19, 1914)

September 29

Wage war against Satan, whether he comes directly with his malicious suggestions or indirectly through the world and our corrupt nature. Cause an uproar with that miserable apostate, and do not worry about his threats to swallow you up at times. It does not matter, because he can do nothing to your soul that Jesus is now holding so close to himself and is upholding in a hidden way with his ever vigilant grace. Cheer up, beloved daughter of Jesus, because I am telling you the truth. Never in the past have things been as good with your soul as they are now.

Do not let yourself think that your sufferings are being inflicted in reparation for your wrongdoings, because the Lord is afflicting you only to embellish your crown with the jewels he has decided to give you.

(To Raffaelina Cerase, September 19, 1914)

September 30

Do not be in doubt about receiving divine assistance, and do not lean on yourself to deal with these multiple afflictions that constantly surround you. Everything will turn out for the glory of God and the salvation of your soul. Tell me, how can you doubt my reassurances? Without divine grace would you have been able in the past to get through so many crises and so many wars? Therefore be confident at all times, because that same grace will still be there for you. You will be saved, and the enemy will gnash his teeth in his rage.

In the meantime continue to pray, to thank God, and to suffer according to his divine purposes and his divine will. Be encouraged by the thought that your reward is not far off.

(To Raffaelina Cerase, April 20, 1915)

OCTOBER

October 1

I see, my dearest daughter, that all the seasons of the year are found in your soul. At times you feel the winter of great sterility, distraction, listlessness, and irritation. You feel the dew of the month of May with its perfume of good little flowers; their summer colors are your desires to please the Lord. That leaves autumn, in which, as you know, we do not see much new fruit. However, it very often happens that at the time of threshing the wheat and pressing the grapes, greater harvests are had than the harvesters and grape harvesters expected.

You would like it always to be spring and summer, daughter, but no. There need to be these vicissitudes in the inner life as there are outside in nature. Only in heaven will everything be as beautiful as spring, as pleasant as autumn, and as full of love as summer. There will be no winter there, but winter is needed here for the discipline of self-denial and for the thousands of small, beautiful virtues that are practiced during times of sterility.

(To Maria Gargani, May 18, 1918)

October 2

My good daughter, keep walking at the same pace, and do not worry if it seems slow to you. If you have good and resolute intentions, you can do nothing but advance in a good way. No, my most beloved daughter, in your practice of virtue you do not need to be always actively attentive to everything. That would actually entangle you and take up too much of your thoughts and affections.

In conclusion, you can and must stay peaceful because the Lord is with you, and it is precisely he who is at work in you. Do not fear remaining in the boat in which he has placed you and left you. Abandon yourself entirely into the arms of our heavenly Father's divine goodness. Do not be afraid, because your fear would be even sillier than a baby's fear in the lap of its mother.

(To Maria Gargani, May 18, 1918)

October 3

May Jesus always be everything to you, and may our father St. Francis reward you for the good you are trying to do for the people of our country as you enlist them to fight under his holy banner. You cannot imagine how much pleasure and consolation I have felt to see the religious reawakening among Third Order Franciscans.

I have wept with emotion and consolation, and many times, in the silence of the night and in the privacy of my little cell, I have lifted up my hand to bless all of you and present all of you to Jesus and to our common father, St. Francis, so that you will be considered his elect offspring and so that through you many other souls would be called—souls who, poor dears, have strayed from the path of righteousness and holiness and whose faith is exhausted and spent. They are scattered like meteors that are dispersed throughout the sky and disappear after losing their way. The star of the Baby Jesus also shines for these souls and leads them back to himself, the one Shepherd and Father of all.

(To Violante Masone, December 31, 1921)

October 4

My dearest daughter,

May Jesus always be everything to you. May he watch over you with a benevolent eye, and may he always help you with everything through his vigilant grace. May he always and in all things be your escort, your support, and your guide, and may he make you holy!

With these sincerest prayers that I regularly lift up to Jesus for you, I am replying to your message sent through Miss Serritelli. I am happy to know that you are still full of good intentions, and I give heartfelt thanks to God for that. Always make more of an effort to use the talents you have received from God.

Earnestly labor for the salvation of our brothers and sisters, and make everyone aware of the spirit of St. Francis, which is the spirit of Jesus Christ. Society needs to be reformed, and I do not know of a more effective method than having everyone become members of the Third Order of St. Francis and live according to his spirit.

(To Elena Bandini, January 25, 1914)

October 5

Be firm in your resolutions. Stay in the boat the Lord has placed you in, and when the storm comes, you will not perish. It may seem to you that Jesus is sleeping, but it only seems that way. Do you not know that even if he sleeps his heart is watching over you regularly? It does not matter if he is sleeping, for at the right time he will get up to restore calm to you. Our very dear St. Peter, Scripture says, was terrified and trembling as he exclaimed, "Lord, save me," and Our Lord took him by the hand and said, "O you of little faith, why did you doubt?" [Matthew 14:30, 31]....

Oh daughter of little faith, what are you afraid of? Isn't he watching over you? You are walking on the sea, and you see the winds and the waves, but isn't Jesus' presence with you enough? What is there for you to fear? But if fear does come upon you, cry out loudly, "Lord, save me," and he will stretch out his hand to you. Hold onto it tightly, and walk cheerfully on the sea of life's storms.

(Unknown addressee, December 27, 1917)

October 6

Live a quiet life, my dearest daughter. Cast out of your imagination whatever could dismay you, and tell Our Lord often, "Oh God, you are my God, and I trust in you; you will help me and be my refuge; I will fear nothing." Not only are you with him, but you are in him and he is in you. What can a child in the arms of such a Father fear? Be like a little child, my most beloved Erminia. Children do not ever think about their future, because they have someone else to think about it for them. They are fearless only when they are with their father. Do the same thing here, my dearest daughter, and be at peace.

(To Erminia Gargani, April 23, 1918)

October 7

People who do not love God are not concerned about God at all and do not even experience fear about not loving him. They do not even bother to think about God with a sincere desire to love him. Even if the thought of God comes to mind at times, they immediately, or almost immediately, brush that thought aside.

Be comforted, I repeat, that as long as you are afraid of not loving God and of offending him, you already do love him and are not offending him in the least. Oh, that it would please heaven for all souls to experience the fear you feel! Then the offense to the Lord would be banished from the face of the earth! We would no longer see so many souls lacking in love for God!… We would lose even the concept of sin among human beings, and we would envisage it only in regard to those disgraced angelic spirits who are fallen and stripped of their dignity.

(To Raffaelina Cerase, March 4, 1915)

October 8

Being subjected to a trial is not under a soul's control at all, and no one can directly do anything to be subjected to a trial; it depends exclusively on God's will. I advise you to remain peaceful and not to be the least bit concerned about what will happen. Everything will be resolved to the glory of God and the sanctification of your soul.

… Give infinite freedom to the action of divine grace in you, and let it always serve to be for his glory and for the salvation of your soul and the souls of others. Never forget that heavenly favors are granted not only for your sanctification but also for the sanctification of others.

(To Raffaelina Cerase, February 23, 1915)

October 9

Let us rejoice that the day is coming when we will sing more joyful hymns to our sweetest Lover, who is the very sweet resting place of all hearts that are in love with him. Let us rejoice, I tell you, for that day is coming, and I hope for it, when our hearts will no longer be suffering the cruel regret of not loving our sweet Lord enough.

Meanwhile, let us prepare ourselves for that great day. If we really love Jesus, let us dust ourselves off once and for all, and let everything that is of this world be removed far from us. Let us seriously ponder in our hearts that, according to St. Paul, all the sufferings of this life are not in any way equal to the great glory that awaits us [see Romans 8:18].

(To Raffaelina Cerase, September 7, 1915)

October 10

Why is it that you think you do not know how to conform yourselves to the divine will? Why do you let yourselves believe that you are nearly deprived of your shepherd just because he is far away in body, although very close in spirit? Come now, my dearest daughters, this is the time to leave behind that kind of spiritual infancy and let your spirits soar into a higher region and breathe purer air there....

I bless God in a heartfelt way that he has made me get to know such truly good people as yourselves and to preach to you that you are God's vineyard. The cistern is faith; the tower is hope; the winepress is holy charity; the surrounding fence is the law of God that separates you from the people of this age.

(To the Ventrella sisters, May 1, 1918)

October 11

My dearest daughters, I tell you that your well-disposed wills are the vineyard. Your cistern consists of the holy inspirations for perfection that God rains down from heaven. Your tower is holy chastity, a tower made of ivory like the tower of David. Your winepress is obedience, which brings great merit for the actions that it presses out. Your fence consists of your vows and aspirations.

May God preserve this vineyard that he has planted with his own hands, my daughters. May God always pour out an abundance of the life-giving waters of his grace into your cistern. May God always be the one to protect your tower. May God be the one who always turns the winepress to press out your good wine. May God keep the beautiful fence surrounding this vineyard impenetrable and shut, and may he make the angels be its eternal vinedressers.

(To the Ventrella sisters, May 1, 1918)

October 12

Here is what the church fathers have to say when exhorting souls to read [holy books]. St. Bernard, in his ladder of perfection, says there are four ways or steps by which to climb up toward God and perfection: reading, meditation, prayer, and contemplation. To bolster what he says, he quotes from the divine Master: "Seek, and you will find; knock, and it will be opened to you" [Matthew 7:7]. Applying those words to the four ways or steps to perfection, he says that one seeks God in the reading of sacred Scripture and holy, devout books. With meditation one finds God, with prayer one knocks at his heart, and with contemplation one enters into the great theater of divine beauty that was opened up precisely through reading, meditation, and prayer.

(To Raffaelina Cerase, July 28, 1914)

October 13

I want you to see how powerful sacred reading can be to induce a change in people's direction and to make even worldly people begin their journey to perfection. For that reason you need merely to reflect on the conversion of St. Augustine. Who conquered that great man for God? In the end the last conqueror was neither his mother with her tears nor the great St. Ambrose with his divine eloquence. Rather it was precisely a reading from the Scriptures.

Whoever reads Augustine's *Confessions* cannot hold back the tears. What an excruciating war! What a fierce conflict his heart had to endure for the great aversion he felt in having to abandon the lewd pleasures of the senses. He says of himself that he was compelled to groan because his will was bound by a strong chain and that the infernal enemy was restricting his will with the shackles of crude needs. He says he experienced the agony of death in separating himself from his depraved habits.

(To Raffaelina Cerase, July 28, 1914)

October 14

However, while Augustine was being assaulted by such tumultuous feelings, he heard a voice that said, "Take and read." He immediately obeyed that voice, and reading from a chapter in St. Paul, the dark fog was cleared from his mind; all the hardness of his heart was softened, and his spirit came into complete serenity and peaceful calm. From that moment on, having broken with the world, the flesh, and the devil, he dedicated everything to the service of God, and then became that great saint who is honored today....

Now, if the reading of holy books has so much power that it can transform worldly people into spiritual ones, can you imagine how powerful such reading can be for spiritual people in leading them to greater perfection?

(To Raffaelina Cerase, July 28, 1914)

October 15

You tell me that venerable [now saint] Sr. Thérèse of the Child Jesus used to say that she did not want to make the choice of living or dying but wanted Jesus to do whatever he wanted with her. Unfortunately, I see all too well that this is a depiction of all the souls that have emptied themselves and are filled up with God. How far my soul is from being emptied that way! I am not successful in curbing my heart impulses, yet I do try, my father, to conform myself to what venerable Sr. Thérèse said, which is actually what every soul passionately in love with God should say....

It is important to be clear here. If the one who is working in me is the same one working in Sr. Thérèse, then her saying should also be mine. Now tell me, don't I have reason to doubt that? Alas! Who will deliver me from such a cruel torment in my heart?

(To Fr. Agostino of San Marco in Lamis, October 17, 1915)

October 16

I can accept, Oh my God, all the torments of this earth gathered into one bundle; I desire that as my portion. However, I could never resign myself to being separated from you because of my lack of love. Oh! Out of pity do not allow my poor soul to stray. Never consent to the failing of my hope. Cause me never to separate myself from you, and if I am separated from you right now without knowing it, drag me back this very instant....

Never allow me, dear Jesus, to lose the very precious treasure you are to me. My Lord and my God, the ineffable sweetness that radiates from your eyes is so vivid to my soul.

(To Fr. Agostino of San Marco in Lamis, October 17, 1915)

October 17

You can see that my poor soul cannot bear the cruel torment of your abandonment, because you have made my soul fall too much in love with you, Infinite Beauty.

You know how my soul is frantically seeking you. My fretting is no less than what your bride in the Song of Solomon felt. My soul, just like that sacred bride, went out into the public streets and squares and implored the daughters of Jerusalem to tell her where to find her beloved:

> I adjure you, O daughters of Jerusalem,
>   if you find my beloved,
> that you tell him
>   I am sick with love. [Song of Solomon 5:8]
>   *(To Fr. Agostino of San Marco in Lamis, October 17, 1915)*

October 18

How well my soul in its current state understands what is written in the Psalms: "My spirit faints" [Psalm 77:3], and, "My soul languishes for your salvation" [Psalm 119:81].

You alone see what grief this is for the soul that is seeking you, my Lord. Yet my soul could bear that grief peacefully out of love for you if only I knew that in this current state I am not abandoned by you, Oh Fountain of eternal happiness!…

Oh! You know what cruel martyrdom it is for my soul to see the great offenses that people commit in these very sad times, to see the horrifying ingratitude with which you are repaid for your loving promises, to see the little thought, if any, that these truly blind people give to their loss of you.

(To Fr. Agostino of San Marco in Lamis, October 17, 1915)

October 19

Oh holy souls who, now free of every worry, are already beatified in heaven in that flowing stream of supreme sweetness, how I envy your happiness! Oh! For pity's sake, since you are so close to the fountain of life and since you see me dying of thirst in this vile world, mercifully grant me some of that most refreshing water....

Beatified souls, be gracious to me and come to my assistance. Since I cannot find what my soul needs for rest at night, I too will rise up like the bride in the Song of Solomon and look for the one I love: "I will seek him whom my soul loves" [Song of Solomon 3:2]. I will always search for him. I will search for him everywhere, and nothing will stop me until I have found him again at the threshold of his kingdom.

(To Fr. Agostino of San Marco in Lamis, October 17, 1915)

October 20

Oh God! Oh God! Where do my thoughts fly? What will become of these wretched children of yours, who are still my brethren, who have already warranted your wrath? You know, my sweet Redeemer, how often the memory of your divine face displaying indignation toward my wretched brethren has made my blood run cold in terror, more so even than the thought of eternal torments and all the pains of hell.

I have always implored you with trembling, the way I implore you now, that through your mercy you would deign to withdraw your wrathful gaze from my wretched brethren.... You have said yourself, my sweet Lord, that "love is strong as death" [Song of Solomon 8:6]. Therefore look up on my lifeless brothers with an eye of ineffable sweetness, binding them to yourself with the strong grip of love.

(To Fr. Agostino of San Marco in Lamis, October 17, 1915)

October 21

This is what ordinarily happens to me during prayer. I hardly set out to pray when suddenly I sense my soul beginning to recollect itself in a peace and tranquillity that I cannot put into words. My senses remain suspended, with the exception of my hearing, which is often not suspended because generally that sense does not distract me, and I must say that even when a lot of noise is going on around me, that does not bother me in the least.

This will help you understand that rarely do I pray by using my mind.

Frequently, at certain moments when I am continuing to think about God—who is always present to me—I distance myself a bit from my mind, and all at once I feel Our Lord touch the center of my soul in a rather penetrating and gentle way. Most of the time I feel compelled to weep tears of sorrow for my unfaithfulness and tears of tenderness for having such a good Father who is so attentive to summon me into his presence.

(To Fr. Benedetto of San Marco in Lamis, November 1, 1913)

October 22

At other times, instead I find myself in great dryness of spirit. I feel my body under great oppression due to my many ailments, and I find it impossible to center myself to pray no matter how great my desire is to do so.

This state of affairs intensifies to the point that it is a miracle from the Lord that I do not die. Then, when it pleases the heavenly Bridegroom of souls to end this martyrdom, in an instant he infuses such devotion into my spirit that I can in no way resist it. I find myself completely changed in the blink of an eye, enriched with supernatural grace and so full of power that I could challenge all of Satan's kingdom.

(To Fr. Benedetto of San Marco in Lamis, November 1, 1913)

October 23

Many times I feel myself overcome by a powerful impulse; I feel my whole self longing so much for God that it seems I could die. This is all the result not of some kind of meditation but of an internal flame and such an excessive love that if God did not quickly come to my assistance, I would indeed be consumed.

In the past, sometimes I used to succeed in calming these impulses, but now I cannot defend myself from them at all. What I can sincerely say about all this is that I am in no way looking for it. I feel at those times that my soul ardently desires to leave this life, and when that desire is denied, I suffer pain that is very acute but at the same time so wonderful that I would never want to have it stop.

(To Fr. Benedetto of San Marco in Lamis, November 1, 1913)

October 24

Sometimes a great desire comes over me to serve the Lord perfectly. There is then no torment that my soul would not suffer gladly. This too happens to me without my seeking it, and it also happens in an instant. I do not understand where such great courage is coming from.

Such desires wear my soul down because, through a very clear light that God sends, I understand that I am unable to render to God the service he would like. Then everything concludes with delights with which God inundates my soul.

(To Fr. Benedetto of San Marco in Lamis, November 1, 1913)

October 25

Most of the time it is painful for me to have conversations with people except for those people I can talk to about God and the infinite value of the soul. Precisely for that reason I prefer solitude.

Very often I experience it as a great burden to attend to the necessities of life: eating, drinking, sleeping, and I submit myself to it like a condemned man, only because God wills that I do these things.

Time seems to fly by quickly, and there is never enough time to pray. I have great affection for good books, but I read very little because I am hindered by my ailments and also because shortly after I open a book and begin to read, I find myself deeply engrossed, and then reading turns into prayer.

When the Lord does these things to me, I feel so completely changed that I no longer recognize myself as who I was before.

(To Fr. Benedetto of San Marco in Lamis, November 1, 1913)

October 26

I know clearly that if there is any good in me it has all come from these supernatural blessings. I realize this is the source of my very firm determination to suffer everything with resignation and readiness without ever growing weary of suffering, although, alas! I do it so imperfectly. I have a very firm resolution not to offend God, even venially. I would suffer death by fire a thousand times before consciously committing any kind of sin....

If conversations just to pass the time are prolonged, and I am unable to get away from them, I have to struggle violently to stay, and they cause me great pain.

(To Fr. Benedetto of San Marco in Lamis, November 1, 1913)

October 27

I would never have had all these supernatural occurrences unless they produced noteworthy benefits for me. In addition to the effects particular to each grace, these heavenly favors have produced three principal effects: a wonderful knowledge of God and his incomprehensible greatness; a deep self-knowledge and a sense of humility in recognizing my great impudence in offending such a holy Father; and a great disdain for the things of this world as well as great love for God and for virtue.

I know my very great desire to associate with people who have most availed themselves of the ways of perfection is part of these heavenly treasures. I love these people very much, because it seems to me they help me love the Author of all wonders, God.

(To Fr. Benedetto of San Marco in Lamis, November 1, 1913)

October 28

Earlier I was experiencing confusion that other people might know what the Lord was doing in me, but for some time now I no longer feel this confusion, because I see that these favors do not mean I am a better person. In fact, I see myself instead as worse because I take so little advantage of all these graces. The concept I have of myself is that I am not sure if there are others who are worse than I am....

All of the above is what my soul ordinarily experiences. However, sometimes it happens, although rarely, that for different periods of time and even on different days these favors are removed from me, and they are so completely blotted out of my mind that I cannot recall the least little good thing that has been in me. It seems my spirit is completely surrounded by darkness and I cannot remember anything at all.

(To Fr. Benedetto of San Marco in Lamis, November 1, 1913)

October 29

Physical and spiritual ailments conspire together to torment me. I feel turmoil in my spirit. I try to form one single thought about God—I cannot say "try to pray" because that would be going too far—but in my current state that is entirely impossible. Then I see that I am full of imperfections. All the courage I had earlier leaves me completely. I become very weak in practicing virtue and in resisting the enemy's assaults. I then become convinced more than ever that I am good for nothing. A deep sadness comes over me, and the horrid thought crosses my mind that I could be deluded without knowing it. Only God knows what torture this is for me! I think to myself, couldn't the Lord, as punishment for my infidelities, allow me unknowingly to deceive myself and my spiritual directors?…

When I am in this state, what I can say for certain is that I do not offend God more than usual because, thank heaven, I never lose my trust in him. On the next visit the Lord pays me, all of this vanishes: My mind is filled with light, I feel my strength and all my good desires revive again, and I even feel a great easing of my physical ailments.

(To Fr. Benedetto of San Marco in Lamis, November 1, 1913)

October 30

Do not give sadness any room in your soul, because that impedes the free operation of the Holy Spirit. If we are going to be sad, let us be sad, but let it be entirely a holy sadness in seeing the evil that is spreading even more throughout today's society. Oh, how many poor souls are daily turning away from God, our Supreme Good!

Not wanting to submit one's judgment to that of others, especially to someone who is very expert in the things in question, is a sign of a lack of docility; it is a very clear indicator of secret pride. You know that, and you agree with me about that. Well, pluck up your courage; avoid falling into that again. Constantly be on the lookout for that accursed vice, knowing how much it displeases Jesus, because it is written that "God opposes the proud, but gives grace to the humble" [James 4:6].

(To Raffaelina Cerase, November 26, 1914)

October 31

My father, if it were not for the war that the devil is constantly waging against me, I would almost be in paradise. I find myself in the devil's hands as he tries to rip me out of Jesus' arms. My God, what a war he is waging! At certain times I am almost on the verge of losing my mind because of the continual violence I have to do to myself. How many tears, how many sighs, my father, do I direct to heaven to be freed of this! But that is not really important, since I will never grow weary of praying to Jesus. It is true that my prayers are more deserving of punishment than of reward because I displeased Jesus so much with my countless sins. In the end he will be moved to have pity on me, either by removing me out of this world and calling me home or by freeing me. And if neither of those two graces is given to me, I at least hope that he will continue to give me the grace not to give in to temptation.

(To Fr. Benedetto of San Marco in Lamis, December 20, 1910)

<h1>NOVEMBER</h1>

November 1

As an inspiration for us to suffer willingly the tribulations that divine mercy bestows on us, let us keep our gaze fixed firmly on the heavenly home that awaits us. Let us contemplate it and set our sights on it, gazing at it incessantly with rapt attention. In addition, let us cease gazing at the goods we see—I am speaking of earthly goods—because the sight of them entrances and distracts the soul and seduces the heart, and they deflect our gaze from being entirely fixed on our heavenly homeland.

Let us listen to what the Lord tells us about this issue through the words of St. Paul the apostle: "We look not to the things that are seen but to the things that are unseen" [2 Corinthians 4:18]. Let us not look at the things that are visible but at the things that are invisible. It is entirely appropriate for us to contemplate heavenly goods and not care about earthly goods, because the former are eternal and the latter are transient.

(To Raffaelina Cerase, October 10, 1914)

November 2

What would we say if we were in front of a poor peasant who became transfixed in contemplating a river that was flowing by very quickly? We would probably laugh, and we would be right to do so. Isn't it foolish to set our gaze on something that is passing by rapidly? This is the very situation of people who fix their gaze on visible goods. What are those goods essentially? Do they differ from a rapid river whose water, as soon as it is seen, flows out of sight never to be seen again?

Let us leave the desire for and love of earthly, material goods behind, my dear, to those who through their own misfortune lack faith; let us leave that desire to the people who unfortunately can no longer discern the precious from the vile. As for us, who have been called through the goodness of God to rule with the divine Bridegroom and in whose minds the true light of God still shines, let us constantly fix our gaze on the splendors of the heavenly Jerusalem.

May our meditation on the many blessings that are to be had up above be the sweet pasture in which our thoughts graze.

(To Raffaelina Cerase, October 10, 1914)

November 3

Oh, how burdensome is this mortal life for the children of God, my dearest daughters, but, oh God, how desirable is the life that is beyond, which the mercy of the Lord will be pleased to grant us! We should not be the least bit doubtful about possessing it one day, even though we are unworthy, and if we are not completely unworthy, that is only because God exercises mercy toward those who have placed their hope in him. When St. Charles Borromeo was at the end of his life, he carried a crucifix with him to make his departure sweeter by gazing on the death of Our Lord.

The best remedy, then, whenever you find yourself in some kind of trial, be it material or moral, physical or spiritual, is to think of the One who is our life and to never think about the trial without also thinking of him.

(To the Ventrella sisters, March 8, 1918)

November 4

Try your best, without excessive anxiety, my daughters, to do with perfection what you ought and what you would like to do. Once you have done something, however, do not think about it anymore. Instead, think only about what you still must do, or would like to do, or are doing right then. Walk in the ways of the Lord with simplicity, and do not torment yourselves. You should despise your shortcomings but with calm rather than with anxiety and restlessness. For that reason, be patient about them and learn to benefit from them in holy self-abasement....

God wants to speak to you through the thorns, the burning bush, the clouds, the lightning, as he did with Moses, but we prefer him to speak to us through a sweet, gentle breeze as he did with Elijah. But what do you fear, daughters? Listen to Our Lord as he speaks to Abraham as well as to us: "Fear not,... I am your shield" [Genesis 15:1].

(To the Ventrella sisters, March 8, 1918)

November 5

Oh! How bitter is the thought of having to account to God for sins we made others commit because of our careless behavior or to account for the good that was not done for souls through ignorance or, God forbid, through negligence!... It is true I have always commended myself to God concerning this very important matter, but who can guarantee that I did all that it was my duty to do? My God, my daughter, that is a thorn that is always lodged in the depth of my soul and that tears at me regularly. Oh daughter! Pray fervently that I may fulfill my ministry fruitfully, and share with me something reassuring, if the good Lord allows you.

(To Maria Gargani, April 9, 1918)

November 6

Place yourself often in God's presence, and offer him all your actions and not just your sufferings. I am not opposed to the idea that when you suffer you do not refrain from complaining about it, but I would want you to complain to the Lord in a filial spirit, the way an affectionate young child would with its mother. Provided that it is done lovingly, it is not bad to complain or to seek to be comforted. Do it with love and submission in the arms of God's will. Do not be dismayed if you do not succeed in performing virtuous actions in the manner you would like, because, as I have told you, your actions do not fail to be good and pleasing to his Divine Majesty, even if they are done—without any sin on your part—without enthusiasm, or in a burdened way, or by sheer force of will.

(Unknown addressee, June 3, 1917)

November 7

My God, what has my life been before you these days, when thickest darkness has completely covered me? What kind of a future do I still have? I understand nothing, absolutely nothing. Meanwhile I will not cease lifting up my hands to your holy sanctuary during the night, and I will always bless you as long as any breath of life remains in me.

I beseech you, my good God, to be my life, my ship, and my harbor. You have made me climb up onto the cross of your Son, and I am trying to adapt myself there in the best possible way. I am convinced that I will never come down and that I will never see the clear, bright air again....

I am open to whatever you wish, but will you let me see you one day on Tabor in a holy illumination? Will I have the tireless strength to ascend to the heavenly vision of my Savior?

(To Fr. Benedetto of San Marco in Lamis, November 8, 1916)

November 8

I feel the ground giving way under me. Who will reinforce my steps? Who except you will support me in my weakness? *Miserere*, have mercy on me, oh God, have mercy on me! Do not make me experience my weakness any longer!…

May faith illumine my mind again; may your charity rekindle this heart that is broken from the pain of offending you in my hour of trial!…

Forgive me, my father! I am no longer able to organize my thoughts. If I had not been interrupted in my writing at this point, I do not know where this letter would have led. I would have unknowingly put your patience severely to the test.

If you would be kind enough to hear about my current condition, I promise I will do it briefly. The war has started up again with more fierceness. For several days my spirit has been plunged into the thickest darkness. I find myself entirely unable to do good. I find myself in a state of extreme abandonment.

(To Fr. Benedetto of San Marco in Lamis, November 8, 1916)

November 9

I am going through a terrible crisis, and I do not know what is in store for me. This crisis is more spiritual than physical, but it is also the case that the physical side experiences and participates in all the spiritual sufferings in an extraordinary way; the spiritual and physical compete to make me suffer pain.

Alas! Who will rescue me from this dark prison? Who will deliver me from this body of death? Blessed be God in the highest heaven! He is my strength, he is my soul's health, he is my eternal portion. I hope in him, I trust in him, and I will fear no evil.

(To Raffaelina Cerase, July 14, 1915)

November 10

Do not say that you are all alone in climbing up to Calvary or that you are all alone in your battle and in your grief, because Jesus is with you and will never abandon you….

For heaven's sake, I beg you to calm your anxieties and your apprehensions. Live quietly and go forward at all times. Let the assurance that I give you from our sweet Lord, the assurance that you are about halfway to the summit of your Calvary, keep you moving ahead. It is true that you are experiencing a very dark night, but let the thought of a clear dawn and a more radiant midday sustain you, hearten you, renew your courage, and encourage you always to advance. Have no doubt that the One who has sustained you up to this point will continue to sustain you at all times with greater and greater patience and divine kindness for the rest of your bitter and difficult journey.

(To Raffaelina Cerase, July 14, 1915)

November 11

What God wants from you is always just and good. Blessed be God forever! Let us set our hand to the plow; in heaven we will have no other role than fulfilling God's will. Let us strive to bless the Lord in the humiliation and the scorn through which we have become a sign to others. Let us bless him in the tribulations of our spirits and in the torments of our hearts, because everything has been ordained by God in his deep wisdom in a very particular way and is being accomplished in you through the heavenly Father's special partiality for you. May he be blessed at all times in all our troubles and in all our sorrows.

Bless him in all that he makes you suffer here below, and rejoice.

(To Raffaelina Cerase, August 15, 1914)

November 12

To succeed in reaching our ultimate goal, we need to follow our divine leader, who leads an elect soul only on the path that he walked himself, the path of self-denial and the cross: "If any man would come after me, let him deny himself and take up his cross and follow me" [Matthew 16:24]. Shouldn't you consider yourself fortunate for being treated this way by Jesus? The person who does not penetrate the secret of the cross is a fool.

The Holy Spirit tells us that to reach the harbor of salvation, the souls of the elect need to go through the fire of painful humiliation and purify themselves, like gold and silver in the crucible, and in that way they spare themselves having to do expiation in the next life:

> Accept whatever is brought upon you,
>> and endure it in sorrow;
>> in changes that humble you be patient.
> For gold and silver are tested in the fire,
>> and acceptable men in the furnace of humiliation.
> [Sirach 2:4–5]

Jesus wants to make us saints at any cost, but more than anything he wants to sanctify you.

(To Raffaelina Cerase, August 15, 1914)

November 13

Always have before the eyes of your mind the gentleness of the divine Master as a prototype and example. According to what the apostle said to the Corinthians, the gentleness of Jesus Christ is on a par with the meekness that was his special virtue and almost his special characteristic: "I, Paul, myself entreat you, by the meekness and gentleness of Christ" [2 Corinthians 10:1]. Shape all your external acts to be in line with that perfect model, so that they may be a faithful mirror of your inner sentiments....

Yes, let us try to imitate, insofar as we can, his gentle, loving actions, and let us try, as much as possible, to make ourselves resemble him on earth, so that we can then be made more perfect and more like him for all eternity in the heavenly Jerusalem.

(To Annita Rodote, July 25, 1915)

November 14

What you need to do when Jesus in his goodness wants to test your faithfulness is to show yourself ready at all times to perform your duties and not to omit doing the things you were used to doing in times of consolation and prosperity. Give no thought to your lack of sensible feelings. Palpable consolation is merely incidental and many times could be harmful for a soul. Serving God without feeling any consolation is what constitutes essential and genuine devotion. It indicates serving and loving God for the sheer sake of loving him.

(To Raffaelina Cerase, July 14, 1914)

November 15

Help yourself the most at this time through spiritual reading. I heartily desire that you read such books all the time, because they are nourishment for your soul and greatly advance you on the path to perfection no less than prayer and meditation do. In prayer and meditation we speak to the Lord, whereas in holy reading it is God who speaks to us. Try to treasure spiritual reading as much as you can, and you will very soon experience a renewal of your spirit.

Before reading these books, lift your mind up to the Lord and ask him to guide your mind and to deign to speak to your heart and to move your will. But that is not enough. You must also declare to the Lord before you begin reading and from time to time during your reading that you are not doing this for the purpose of studying or satisfying your curiosity but only to please him.

(To Raffaelina Cerase, July 14, 1914)

November 16

I ask you again and again, calm your anxieties concerning your fear of offending God and not knowing how to please him. Believe the assurance from my authority to speak to you on God's behalf that in whatever way you act—as long as you clearly know your actions are not contrary to God's will and to the will of the appropriate authorities—Jesus is always pleased with you if your actions are directed to God's glory.

You need to act according to this guideline without hesitation or argument. You need to move ahead, doing your work without listening to the voice of your fears. Note, my good daughter, I said *listen*, that is, to give heed to, to pay attention to, and so on. I am not saying *hear* because it is impossible not to hear those fears, but do not pay attention to any of them.

(To Maria Gargani, March 30, 1917)

November 17

While this trial lasts, I know that you…do not understand the reason for it and do not have the experiential comfort of this great truth [that the Lord is pleased with you]. However, obey the voice of the one who loves your soul before God as much as his own soul, and let that be sufficient. God told the holy virgin Gertrude one day that he wanted his elect souls to be convinced of the truth that he was very pleased with their prayers and good deeds when they served him at their own expense. Serving him at a cost consists in faithfully saying one's prayers and doing devotions to the best of one's ability while not sensing any feelings of delight in devotion whatsoever and trusting that the Lord in his goodness will accept all of it gladly.

(To Maria Gargani, March 30, 1917)

November 18

Tell me, is it possible that Jesus is far from you when you are calling on him, praying to him, seeking him, and—I say it plainly—when you already possess him? Is it possible that a soul who is on the cross with him, is it possible, I ask, for God not to be in that soul when he has given his infallible word that he would be with that soul in its tribulations: "I will be with him in trouble" [Psalm 91:15]? How is it possible that the fountain of living water that flows from the divine heart could be far from a soul who runs to it like a thirsty deer? It is true that a soul might not believe that to be the case because it is beset by an inextinguishable and insatiable thirst. But what of it? Is that really an argument that the soul does not possess God? Just the opposite.

(To Raffaelina Cerase, October 21, 1915)

November 19

A soul can feel this insatiable thirst because it has not yet reached the end of its journey; it has not yet been fully immersed in the eternal fountain of his divine love, which will happen in the kingdom of glory. Therefore let us enjoy quenching our thirst in this fountain of living water, and let us always move forward on the paths of divine love. But, my daughter, we also need to understand that our souls will not be fully satisfied here below. In fact, woe to us if, while we are still running our course, we believe one day that we are fully satisfied, because that would signal that we think we have reached our destination, and we would be deceived.

(To Raffaelina Cerase, October 21, 1915)

November 20

I confess before anything else that it is a great embarrassment to me not to know how to talk about or deal with this burning volcano that is constantly in me, that Jesus has poured into this small heart of mine.

I can summarize it this way: I am consumed by love for God and love for my neighbor. God is fixed in my mind and stamped on my heart at all times; I never lose sight of him. I, for my part, admire his beauty, his smiles, the turmoil he sends me, his mercies, his vengeance—or, I should say, the rigors of his justice.

With this kind of deprivation of my freedom and this binding of my spiritual and physical faculties, imagine how my poor soul is overwhelmed by these sentiments.

(To Fr. Benedetto of San Marco in Lamis, November 20, 1921)

November 21

How is it possible to see God so saddened by evil and not be likewise saddened? When I see God about to unleash his lightning bolts, there is no other way to fend him off except to lift up one hand to hold back his arm and to signal frantically to my brethren with my other hand. I signal them for two reasons: that they cast aside evil and that they move away from their current position because the hand of justice is about to be unleashed against them.

Believe me, however, that at this moment my inner self is not the least bit shaken or changed in any crippling way. I only want to have and want what God wants. I feel myself resting in him at all times, at least internally; externally sometimes I feel a bit uncomfortable.

What about my brethren, then? Alas! How many times, if not always, has it been up to me to say with Moses to God the judge, "Forgive their sin—and if not, blot me, I beg you, out of your book which you have written" [Exodus 32:32]....

Pray for me, my father, for a stream of water to refresh me a bit because of the devouring flames that are burning in my heart without any respite.

(To Fr. Benedetto of San Marco in Lamis, November 20, 1921)

November 22

Oh Raffaelina, how comforting it is for you to know that we are under the care of a celestial spirit who never abandons us (how wonderful!), even when we act in a way that displeases God! How sweet that great truth is for a believing soul! Can the devout soul who makes an effort to love Jesus fear anyone then, when it is always accompanied by such an illustrious warrior? Could he perhaps be one of the many angels who, with the angel St. Michael, defended God's honor in the empire above against Satan and all the other rebellious angels who were dispatched to perdition and relegated to hell?

Well, you need to know that this angel is still powerful against Satan and his satellites. His love has not failed and will never fail to defend us. Cultivate the habit of always thinking about him and realizing that a heavenly spirit is always right next to us. He does not leave us for one instant from the cradle to the grave. He guides and protects us as a friend or a brother would.

(To Raffaelina Cerase, April 20, 1915)

November 23

Be aware, Raffaelina, that this good angel prays for you. He offers all your good deeds and all your holy and pure desires to God. During the times you seem to be alone and abandoned, do not complain about not having a friend you can open up to and with whom you can share your sorrows. For goodness' sake, do not forget this invisible companion who is always there to listen to you and always ready to comfort you.

Oh, what delightful intimacy! Oh, what blessed companionship! Oh, if only everyone knew how to understand and appreciate this great gift: God, in the overabundance of his love for humanity, has assigned this heavenly being to us! Remember his presence often.

(To Raffaelina Cerase, April 20, 1915)

November 24

Invoke this guardian angel often, and often repeat this beautiful prayer: "Angel of God, who guards me and to whom I have been entrusted through the goodness of the heavenly Father, enlighten me, guard me, and guide me now and forever." What consolation it will be for your soul, my dear Raffaelina, at the hour of death to see this good angel who accompanied you throughout your life and was so full of maternal care for you! Oh! May this sweet thought always make you more devoted to the cross of Jesus, since that is precisely what this good angel wants!… How many times, alas, have I made my good angel weep! How many times have I lived without the least fear of offending the purity of his gaze! Oh! He is so gentle, so sensitive! My God, how many times have I responded to this angel's caring concerns that are more than maternal without any sign of respect, affection, and gratitude?

(To Raffaelina Cerase, April 20, 1915)

November 25

The very lofty light that God sends into some souls fills their spirits in a painful and desolating way and causes them extreme affliction and excruciating pain. They are not currently able to understand this divine working, this profound light, for two reasons. The first is that this light is so lofty and sublime that it surpasses the very capacity of their souls and thus causes darkness and torment rather than light. The second reason is due to the baseness and impurity of these souls, which not only obscures the profound light but also causes pain for them instead of comfort. It fills them with pain in their bodies and with grievous agonies and horrendous pain in their spirits.

This is in accord with the principle that when the divine light finds souls that are not yet suited for union with God, it comes into them in a purgative mode. When the light has purged them, then it fills them with illumination, lifting them up to the perfect vision of and union with God.

(To Fr. Agostino of San Marco in Lamis, December 19, 1913)

November 26

We are not all called by God to save souls and to glorify him through the lofty apostolate of preaching. However, understand that this is not the one and only way to reach these two great ideals. A soul can proclaim the glory of God and work for the salvation of souls through a genuine Christian life by praying to the Lord without ceasing, "Thy kingdom come," and by praying that his most holy name be "hallowed," that he "lead us not into temptation," and that he "deliver us from evil" [Matthew 6:9–13].

This is what you should continue doing, while offering yourself constantly to the Lord for these purposes. Pray for the wicked, pray for the lukewarm, pray even for the fervent, but pray especially for the supreme pontiff and all the spiritual and temporal needs of the holy church, our very tender mother. Say a special prayer for all those who labor for the salvation of souls and the glory of God in their missionary work to faithless and unbelieving people.

(To Raffaelina Cerase, April 11, 1914)

November 27

You tell me that because your spirit is sleepy, distracted, fickle, and very abject, in addition to your physical problems many times as well, you cannot manage to stay in church more than an hour and a half. Do not be troubled about that, but try not to do anything to cause that to happen. For your part try to overcome every harassment and annoyance, and do not overly tire yourself with very long, continuous prayers or by praying when your spirit and your mind are unable to do so.

Meanwhile, during the course of the day try to withdraw when you can and, in the silence of your heart and in solitude, offer your praises, your benedictions, your humble and contrite heart, and your whole self to the heavenly Father. This way, while the goodness of the heavenly Bridegroom is being neglected by the majority of creatures made in his image, we will keep ourselves close to him by setting such times aside and by engaging in such practices.

(To Raffaelina Cerase, September 19, 1914)

November 28

Let us not be bewildered, my Raffaelina, during the times of our testing. Through our faithfulness in doing good and through patience in fighting the good fight, we will overcome the impudence of all our enemies, and as the divine Master said, we will conquer our souls through patience because, as St. Paul says, we know that "suffering produces endurance, and endurance produces character, and character produces hope" [Romans 5:3]. Let us follow Jesus on the path of suffering; let us always keep our eyes fixed on the heavenly Jerusalem, and every difficulty that is an obstacle on our journey will be successfully overcome.

(To Raffaelina Cerase, October 14, 1915)

November 29

Let us stir up our faith more and remember that resounding victory of the Israelites over the Midianites recorded in sacred Scripture. We read that in the middle of the night, when the enemy had come out of their trenches and were resting in the camp, suspecting nothing, they were silently surrounded by just three hundred of Gideon's warriors. Each man had a trumpet in one hand and a jar with a lit torch in the other hand. At their captain's signal, they broke the jars with a loud crash and blew their trumpets. After every blast they lifted up their war cry: "For the LORD and for Gideon" [Judges 7:18].

At their tremendous cry, the loud noise of the trumpets, and the immense flash of light in their faces, great terror came upon the enemy camp, and they all began to run in a confused fashion, still heavy with sleep, while the trumpets continued to send out their grim sound. A great number of the enemy, in the indescribable confusion of their hurried flight, massacred one another, leaving mounds of dead bodies in the camp.

The Israelites obtained this victory, as we saw, not with weapons but through a very unique war strategy.

Well, we also are sustaining a difficult war as long as we are alive. Let us win this war with Gideon's very unique strategy. Let us make the light of our good deeds, the virtue of the knowledge of God, and our fervent desire for God's word go before us in this battle. Let us also fight to the sound of hymns, psalms, and spiritual songs as we sing and lift up loud voices to the Lord. In this way we too will be made worthy to win the victory in Jesus Christ Our Lord.

(To Raffaelina Cerase, October 14, 1915)

November 30

Remember that peace can be maintained in one's spirit even in the midst of all the storms of this life. Peace, as you know well, essentially consists in being in harmony with our neighbors and wanting good for them. It also consists in being in friendship with God through his sanctifying grace. The proof of being united to God is the moral certainty that there is no mortal sin weighing our souls down. Peace, finally, consists in having won the victory over the world, the devil, and our own passions.

Tell me now, isn't it true that the peace Jesus brings us can guard us very well not only when our spirits have an abundance of consolations but also when our hearts are immersed in bitterness because of the roaring and shrieking of the enemy?

(To Raffaelina Cerase, October 10, 1914)

December 1

Do not fear; Jesus is with you, and you are with him!…

You have reason to complain, my dearest daughter, because most of the time you find yourself in darkness. You seek God, you sigh, you call on him, and you cannot discover any trace of him. It seems that God is hiding himself, that he has abandoned you! But, I repeat, do not be afraid. Jesus is still with you now, and you are in him and with him. He conceals himself, he hides himself to whet your love. In your darkness, tribulation, and agony, Jesus is with you. My good daughter, you see nothing but darkness in your spirit, but I assure you on behalf of God that the light of the Lord is flooding you and enveloping your spirit.

(To Antonietta Vona, June 28, 1918)

December 2

You think yourself abandoned, but I assure you that Jesus is holding you closer than ever to his divine heart.

Even Our Lord lamented the abandonment of his Father on the cross, but has the Father ever, or could he ever, abandon his Son?… Proclaim your own *fiat*, your "let it be so," in a surrendered way when you find yourself in such trials, and do not fear.…

Write to me often about the state of your soul, and fear nothing. All the love of the one who has a father's heart for you will be applied on your behalf. Although I am unworthy, I pray and have others pray for you all the time. Be content to have Jesus treat you as he wishes, because he is always a very good father!

(To Antonietta Vona, June 28, 1918)

December 3

St. Augustine says it very well when he says that our restless hearts will not rest until they rest in the object of our love.

Now, you know very well that perfect love is obtained only when we possess the object of our love. However, God, the object of the love Augustine is talking about, will be fully possessed only when we see him face-to-face instead of through a veil. As St. Paul says, then we will see him as he is, and we will know him as we know ourselves [see 1 Corinthians 13:12]. This will happen only when the doors of our prison are opened.

Based on this, imagine what the pain of a soul to whom God has revealed some of his heavenly treasures must be when it finds itself still a pilgrim in exile on earth.

(To Raffaelina Cerase, April 20, 1915)

December 4

Our very sweet Jesus is demonstrating love itself to you, not abandonment. It is not the least bit true that due to your current state of spiritual darkness and desolation you are offending God, because his watchful grace is guarding you very well from offending him.

If you are not offending God, and on the contrary are loving him in the state he has chosen for you, what do you need to be upset about? What is there for you to grieve about? Begin, then, your ascent to the cross. Stretch yourself out on it and be patient with yourself, because, as our divine Master tells us, in patience we will conquer and possess our souls. That self-possession will be steadier the less it is mixed with worry and anxiety.

(To Erminia Gargani, December 6, 1916)

December 5

Pluck up your courage and be assured that God is pleased with you and finds his *peaceful dwelling* in you. Do not wait for Tabor to see God. You are already contemplating him on Mount Sinai without realizing it.... Our mental wanderings, our involuntary distractions, temptations, etc., are the wares offered by the enemy, but resist him and then you will do nothing wrong. When the devil causes a fuss, it is an excellent sign, because it means he wants to capture your will, and that means he is still outside of you and external to your will.

(To Erminia Gargani, December 6, 1916)

December 6

Even St. Paul was restless and asked to be relieved of the difficult test in his flesh,...but was he not assured that the help of grace would always be sufficient for him?

Our enemy, who is committed to our harm, wants to convince you otherwise, but spurn him in the name of Jesus and laugh at him. This is the best remedy for beating him into retreat. He becomes emboldened by our weakness, but when someone confronts him with a weapon in hand, he becomes a coward.

(To Raffaelina Cerase, April 25, 1914)

December 7

Flee, flee away from the least whisper that makes you puffed up. Always reflect on and keep before your eyes the great humility of the Mother of God and our mother. To the extent that heavenly gifts increased in her, she deepened her humility even more to the point of being able to say at the very moment she was overshadowed by the Holy Spirit, making her the mother of the Son of God, "Behold, I am the handmaid of the Lord" [Luke 1:38]. Our dear mother proclaimed the same thing in St. Elizabeth's house when she was carrying the Word made flesh in her womb.

(To Raffaelina Cerase, May 13, 1915)

December 8

As your gifts increase, increase your humility, remembering that every-thing has been given to you on loan. May your humble gratitude to such an illustrious benefactor always be joined to any increase in gifts as you burst forth in continual thanksgiving. As you do this you will defy and overcome all of hell's ire, and the forces that oppose you will be crushed. You will be saved, and the enemy will bite himself in rage. Have faith in divine assistance, and be sure that he who has defended you until now will continue his work of salvation in you.

(To Raffaelina Cerase, May 13, 1915)

December 9

Let your normal meditation focus on the life, passion, and death of Our Lord Jesus Christ as well as on his resurrection and ascension. You could meditate on his birth; his flight to Egypt and his time there; his return from Egypt and his hidden life in the workshop in Nazareth until he was thirty years old; his humility in having himself baptized by his precursor, St. John. You could meditate on his public life; his sorrowful passion and death; his institution of the most holy sacrament on that night when people were preparing the most atrocious tortures for him; his prayer in the garden, when he sweat blood at the sight of the torments being prepared for him and because of the ingratitude of the people who had not availed themselves of his merits. You could meditate on Jesus being dragged away and brought before tribunals; Jesus being scourged and crowned with thorns; his journey up the hill of Calvary carrying his cross; his crucifixion; and finally his agonizing death on the cross before the eyes of his very grieved mother.

(To Annita Rodote, March 8, 1915)

December 10

My good sisters and daughters, continue to remember me in the treasury of your prayers, especially during this time of great trial for me. Understand that what is and has been important to me far more than physical health is spiritual health....

In my humble, yes, but fervent prayers, I will not forget you and how much charity you have shown me. May Jesus and the Blessed Virgin make you worthy of eternal glory. With that faith and hope, I wish you every good gift from heaven.

Now I will address your spiritual needs. The confusion of spirit you are experiencing is a spiteful work of the tempter, and God is allowing it not because he hates you but because he loves you. The feelings you have are not objectionable, but your consent to them would be reprehensible. Therefore I exhort you by our most gentle Lord to be tranquil, because neither are you offending the Lord by having these feelings, nor is the Lord hiding himself to punish you for your unfaithfulness. I tell you in the name and power of holy obedience that there is no infidelity in you, since a disloyal action requires full knowledge and premeditation.

(To the Ventrella sisters, December 11, 1916)

December 11

Your yearning for the peace of eternity is good and holy, but it needs to be balanced by complete submission to divine wishes. It is better to do God's will on earth than to have joy in paradise. St. Teresa's motto was that it was better to suffer than to die. Purgatory is sweet when you suffer out of love for God.

The trials that the Lord is giving and will give you are all signs of divine favor and will be jewels for your soul. Dear ones, the winter will pass and eternal spring will arrive, and it will be as rich in beauty as the storms were harsh. The fog that you are experiencing is an indication of God's proximity to you.

(To the Ventrella sisters, December 11, 1916)

December 12

Moses, the great leader of God's people, found the Lord in the cloudy mist at the top of Sinai. The Israelite people saw the mist in the form of a cloud, and it appeared as a cloud in the temple. Jesus Christ, in his transfiguration on Tabor, was at first visible and then became invisible to the apostles when he was enveloped by a luminous cloud. When God hides himself in cloudy mists, that means he is looming larger in your eyes and that he is transfiguring himself from the visible and intelligible to pure divinity....

My comments about cloudy mists should have already answered your question about the shadows that seem to be darkening in you. They are not really shadows, my beloved daughters, they are really light, but a light so strong and penetrating that it dazes the soul that is accustomed to thinking of God in the normal human way. Give thanks to the Lord that even in this life he is disposing you to have a foretaste of that vision by which, seeing nothing, we see everything.

(To the Ventrella sisters, December 11, 1916)

December 13

Be assured that your internal struggles do not pose a danger to your faithfulness to God but are instead an occasion for precious merit—a crown and a victory palm. Do not doubt the goodness of your actions at all, because everything you are doing is being done under obedience, as I have previously told you and I tell you again....

Your obedience does not include, and cannot include, any actions that you clearly know to be offensive to God. Am I being clear? Have you understood me? Do what I have told you, and I will bear the responsibility.

(To the Ventrella sisters, December 11, 1916)

December 14

Continue to be consumed even more by this great longing to please Jesus, and he who is so good and is not a scrupulous taskmaster will reward you for these holy desires by making you grow and advance in his holy ways.

Live completely for him, and always banish useless thoughts that fill your heart with vanity and confuse and cloud your mind.

Be zealous to perform all your actions, even the most insignificant ones, with a strict intention of pleasing God, not caring in the least about their profitability. What richer payment is there for a soul than giving pleasure to the Lord?

Always have a humble assessment of yourself, knowing that your services to God, even if they are many, nonetheless always count for little. If your services garner merit and esteem, that is only because of the grace of the Lord.

(To Annita Rodote, September 12, 1915)

December 15

I am immersed in an ocean of fire. The wound that has opened up again bleeds, and it is always bleeding. That in itself would be enough to make me die more than a thousand times. Oh my God! Why can't I die? Can you not see that the very life that you give me is a torment for my soul? Are you so cruel that you remain deaf to the cries of the one who suffers and you do not comfort him? What am I saying? Forgive me, my father, I am beside myself, and I do not know what I am saying. The excessive pain caused by that open wound makes me wild, although that is against my will. It makes me be beside myself and leads to a frenzy that I cannot control.

Tell me clearly, my father. Am I offending the Lord when I fall into these excesses? What should I do not to displease the Lord if this inner conflict happens automatically and I do not have strength enough to resist? My God! May I soon no longer have a physical life if every effort to be revived from spiritual death is useless! Heaven, it seems, is closed to me, and my every upward impulse and groaning are repaid only by the arrow that fatally wounds my poor heart. My praying seems to get me nowhere!

… I have never had my faculties so locked up and paralyzed. Oh, what bitterness that is for my will, memory, and intellect! I think the pain that my will is suffering—a will that wants to do good or at least desires a willingness to do good—is harsh and inconceivable….

My mind is crushed as though under the press and as such is made blind by it. It is such a painful blindness that only someone who has experienced it could know the extent of it.

(To Fr. Benedetto of San Marco in Lamis, September 5, 1918)

December 16

Take Communion daily, pushing aside irrational doubts at all times. Trust in joyful blind obedience, and do not fear any evil. The wooden plank that carries you into the port of salvation, the divine weapon that leads to victory songs, is complete submission of your judgment to the dictates of the one who is charged with guiding you through the shadows, the perplexities, and the battles of life. Therefore, I repeat, because it is useful to do so, chase away any doubts in the name and power of obedience, and be convinced that you are *not sinning* in this battle. I declare this to you, and that is the truth.

(To the Ventrella sisters, December 11, 1916)

December 17

At the beginning of the sacred novena in honor of the Holy Child Jesus, my spirit felt as though it were reborn to new life. My heart now feels it can contain heavenly blessings. My soul completely melts in the presence of this God who became flesh for us. How can anyone help but love him at all times with new zeal? Oh, let us draw near to Baby Jesus with a pure heart cleansed of sin, so that we may taste how sweet and gentle it is to love him.

I will never fail, but especially during these holy days, to pray to the Holy Paraclete for every human being, and especially for you and all the people you carry in your heart. I will ask him to have you participate in all those charisms that he has so generously poured into my spirit and continues to pour into me more and more.

(To Raffaelina Cerase, December 17, 1914)

December 18

The great good of your soul is to belong wholly and entirely to God. The one who completely belongs to God never grieves except for having offended God. That grief is transformed into a profound but tranquil and peaceful humility and submission, after which the soul is lifted up into divine goodness by a sweet and perfect confidence that is devoid of melancholy or remorse.

The one who completely belongs to God seeks nothing but God himself. Since God is no less present in tribulation than in prosperity, that person can live at peace in the midst of adversities.

The one who completely belongs to God thinks about him continually throughout all of life's events and always tries to improve in God's eyes. That person finds and admires God in all his creatures and exclaims with St. Augustine that all of God's creatures tell us to love him....

Therefore, my dearest daughter, always belong to God and live only in him, desiring only to please him and the creatures in him, through him, and for him.

(To Rachelina Russo, August 17, 1918)

December 19

During the forthcoming celebrations for holy Christmas, with my heart on my lips and with more than filial affection, I send you my sincerest wishes, praying to Baby Jesus for your spiritual and temporal happiness. May the little baby about to be born receive the humble and inadequate prayers that, with a livelier faith during these holy days, I lift up to him for you, for all my superiors, and for the whole world!

May it also please this Heavenly Infant to accept my desires, which are to love him as much as a creature can love him on this earth and to see him loved that way by everybody else!

(To Fr. Agostino of San Marco in Lamis, December 19, 1913)

December 20

May he rain down at last some heavenly dew into the hearts of any afflicted souls! Right now I have no words for them except to say that their condition is enviable. I rejoice in my spirit to see them so shaken and feel a holy envy of them, an envy of wanting to emulate them. Their current condition…, dear father, is such that they are no longer able to experience any kind of comfort, no matter what good words anyone could say to them.

God has plunged their minds into darkness; their wills are in a state of dryness; their minds are empty; their hearts are in bitterness, dejection, and extreme desolation. This is very enviable to me, because all of that is happening to dispose and prepare their hearts to receive the true formation of their spirit, which leads to a union with Love.

(To Fr. Agostino of San Marco in Lamis, December 19, 1913)

December 21

Stay close to the crib of this gracious child, especially during this holy season of his nativity.... Be full of love for this heavenly baby, respectful of your experience with him through prayer and constantly delighting in the joy of sensing in yourself the holy inspirations and affections that come from being singularly his.

Take courage about your minor weaknesses and defects. They will go away, but if they do not, it will be an exercise in humility and mortification for you. Live in peace, my daughter, and do not be afraid, because Jesus is with you. Continue the path you are on, and never slow down.

(To Maria Gargani, December 30, 1918)

December 22

I want to wish you and all your precious family again a wonderful feast of the Holy Child. May Our Lord and the Blessed Virgin make you ever more worthy of eternal glory. With this faith and hope, I wish you all a very happy celebration of the most holy birth of the Child Jesus. I fervently pray that he will grant you the longest life possible and always increase your charity, the queen and mother of all the virtues.

Oh, how sublime is that beautiful virtue of charity that the Son of God brought us! It should be in everyone's heart but even more so in the hearts of those who profess holiness. The Lord has called you to this, not through any of your own merit. Although I see you are well underway in charity, I will not cease to insist that you should advance even more in it.

(To Raffaelina Cerase, December 22, 1914)

December 23

The coldness that you sometimes experience in your spirit should not surprise you, nor should it pull you down or dishearten you, because you do have a genuine desire for fervor. Therefore, do not let the effect of that spiritual coldness derail you from your holy devotions. You are progressing well and are serving God and loving him at a cost to yourself with disinterested love. Tell me, my good daughter, doesn't Jesus initially come to birth in a person's cold heart? Why then would he not stay in a heart that has become cold? I do not mean the coldness that consists in relinquishing our good resolutions; I mean the coldness that consists in a kind of weariness and heaviness of spirit that make it painful for us to walk on the path we have been set on and that we never should leave until we reach our destination.

(Unknown addressee, August 4, 1917)

December 24

May the Child Jesus always reign in your heart and establish and strengthen his kingdom more and more in you. This prayer and others are what I am praying to the Baby of Bethlehem for you during these days.

Our Lord loves you, my daughter; he loves you tenderly. If he does not always have you experience the sweetness of his love, he does that to make you more humble and abject in your own eyes. Do not stop having recourse confidently to his goodness because of this, especially at this time when we see him represented as the tiny infant in Bethlehem. My daughter, for what reason did he become this sweet and lovable baby if not to provoke us to love him with confidence and to trust him lovingly?

(To Antonietta Vona, December 25, 1918)

December 25

May the Child Jesus inspire in you more and more a love for suffering and a disdain for the world. May his star illuminate your mind more and more, and may his love transform your heart and make it worthy of his divine kindness.

With these very sincere prayers that I regularly present to the Child Jesus for you these days, I am replying to your letter that just arrived. May it please Jesus to hear all my prayers for you.

I am glad for the way that grace is leading you, and as I congratulate you, I join with you again in extolling the divine kindness for so much favor being shown to you. Open your heart wide, then, and let the Lord work freely in you. Open your soul to the divine sun, and let its beneficial rays dissipate the darkness that the enemy so often makes denser.

I recommend unquestioning obedience to the one who is standing in for God. The Holy Spirit tells us that the obedient will sing of victory before God. Always consider yourself nothing before the Lord and esteem others highly, especially those who love God better than you do. Rejoice about that because the love that you were not able to give to God is given to him by other souls who are dearer to God and more faithful to him.

(To Maria Gargani, no date)

December 26

Grow at all times and do not become weary of advancing in the queen of all virtues, Christian charity. There is no such thing as too much growth in this wonderful virtue. Consider it very precious, even more than the pupil of your eye, because it is actually the virtue that is dearest to our divine Master, who in his divine words generally calls it "my commandment" [John 15:12]. Oh! Yes, hold this precept of the divine Master in high esteem, and all your difficulties will be overcome.

The virtue of charity is so extremely good, Raffaelina, that the Son of God, specifically to enkindle it in our hearts, descended in person from the bosom of the eternal Parent and made himself like us so he could teach it to us and leave us the means by which to acquire it.

Let us persistently ask Jesus for this virtue and make every effort to grow in it.

(To Raffaelina Cerase, March 30, 1915)

December 27

I urge you to join with me and approach Jesus to receive his embrace, his kiss that sanctifies and saves us.... The prophet Isaiah spoke about a son: "For to us a child is born, / to us a son is given" [Isaiah 9:6].

This child, Raffaelina, is the loving brother, the very loving Bridegroom of our souls whose companionship the bride in the Song of Solomon—who is a metaphor for the faithful soul—was seeking and whose divine kisses she was pining for: "O that you were like a brother to me. / ... / If I met you outside, I would kiss you" [Song of Solomon 8:1]; "O that you would kiss me with the kisses of your mouth" [Song of Solomon 1:2].

This son is Jesus, and the way for us to kiss him without betraying him, to hold him without imprisoning him, the way to kiss him and embrace him with the grace and love that he expects from us and that he promises to return, says St. Bernard, is to serve him with genuine affection and to enact through our holy deeds the heavenly doctrines that we confess with our words.

(To Raffaelina Cerase, September 7, 1915)

December 28

Oh my daughter, who can uncover the wonderful secrets that are hidden beneath the veil of the bride's words [see Song of Solomon 1:2; 8:1]? You would be asking me in vain if you wanted me to explain all those wonderful secrets to you. However, what I can say is that when a soul has been made worthy by our sweetest Lord of saying those very words of the bride, it senses such sweetness that it becomes well aware that Jesus is very close by. All the soul's faculties come into such perfect calm that it seems to possess God as much as it desires. It experiences firsthand the emptiness of all the things of this vile world.

The divine Bridegroom reveals very important truths to that soul in a completely new way. However, the soul does not see this divine Lover who is manifesting himself in this way; it only knows that he is there and cannot doubt that at all. It finds itself in an atmosphere of dazzling light and experiences such wonderful effects of this union with the Bridegroom. The soul feels so established in virtue that it almost seems it no longer is what it was before. Submerged in that ocean of celestial consolation and in that inebriation of joy, it no longer knows what to desire or ask for from God.

In brief, in that wave of light and beatitude, the soul does not know what it has become. It feels completely raptured out of itself. The poor soul feels so tightly held by the divine Bridegroom that it feels as though it will swoon.

(To Raffaelina Cerase, September 7, 1915)

December 29

Another year is passing into eternity with the weight of sins I have committed during that time! How many souls more fortunate than I will salute the new dawn but not the day's end? How many souls will have entered into Jesus' home and remain there for all eternity! How many souls, much happier than I, do I envy for having passed into eternity experiencing the death of the righteous! They were kissed by Jesus, comforted by the sacraments, and assisted by a minister of God; they died with a heavenly smile on their lips despite the torment of physical pain that was oppressing them!

Life here below, my father, is a grief to me. It is such a bitter torment for me to live the life of exile that I can almost no longer bear it. The thought at every instant that I could lose Jesus causes an anxiety that I cannot put into words. Only the soul who sincerely loves Jesus could understand it.

During these days of the feast of the heavenly Child, which are so solemn for me, I have often been seized by these excesses of divine love that make my heart languish so much. In light of all the concessions Jesus has granted me, I have addressed this single prayer to him with more confidence: "Oh Jesus, may I love you, and may I suffer when you desire. May I make you happy and be able to do reparation in some way for the ingratitude of human beings toward you!"

(To Fr. Agostino of San Marco in Lamis, December 29, 1912)

December 30

In all things show yourself more worthy of your vocation as a Christian.

Live in such a way that the heavenly Father can be glorified through you, as so many elect souls like yourself already do. Live in such a way that at every instant you can say with the apostle St. Paul, "Be imitators of me, as I am of Christ" [1 Corinthians 11:1]. Live in such a way, I repeat, that the world can once again say, "Here is the Christ." Oh! Please do not think that expression is exaggerated! Every Christian who is a true imitator and follower of the Nazarene can and should call himself or herself a second Christ, because each carries the imprint of the Lord in a very eminent way. Oh! If all the Christians lived out their vocation, this earth of exile would be transformed into a paradise.

(To Raffaelina Cerase, March 30, 1915)

December 31

I am very cognizant of the fact that there is nothing in me to attract the gaze of our very sweet Jesus. It is only his goodness that has filled my soul with so many blessings. I am hardly ever out of his sight; he follows me everywhere. He restores my life when it is poisoned by sin; he dissipates the thick clouds that surround my soul after sin.

At night when I close my eyes, the veil is lowered and paradise is opened up to me. Comforted by that vision, I sleep with a gentle, beatific smile on my lips and a perfect calm on my brow. I wait for the little companion of my childhood [his guardian angel] to come wake me so that we can lift up morning praises together to our hearts' delight.

(To Fr. Agostino of San Marco in Lamis, October 14, 1912)

About the Editor

Gianluigi Pasquale is a Capuchin of the province of Veneto in Italy. He holds a research doctorate in theology from the Gregorian University in Rome and a research doctorate in philosophy from the Università degli Studi "Ca' Foscari" in Venice. Currently he is a professor at the Lateran Pontifical University in Rome and at the Theological Study Center in Venice, of which he is also president. He has written many works in theology, philosophy, and spirituality.

About the Translator

Marsha Daigle-Williamson received her master's degree in French from the University of Wisconsin and her doctorate in comparative literature from the University of Michigan. She has done translations from French and Italian and is currently professor emeritus of English at Spring Arbor University in Michigan.